EASY
CHEESE
BOARDS

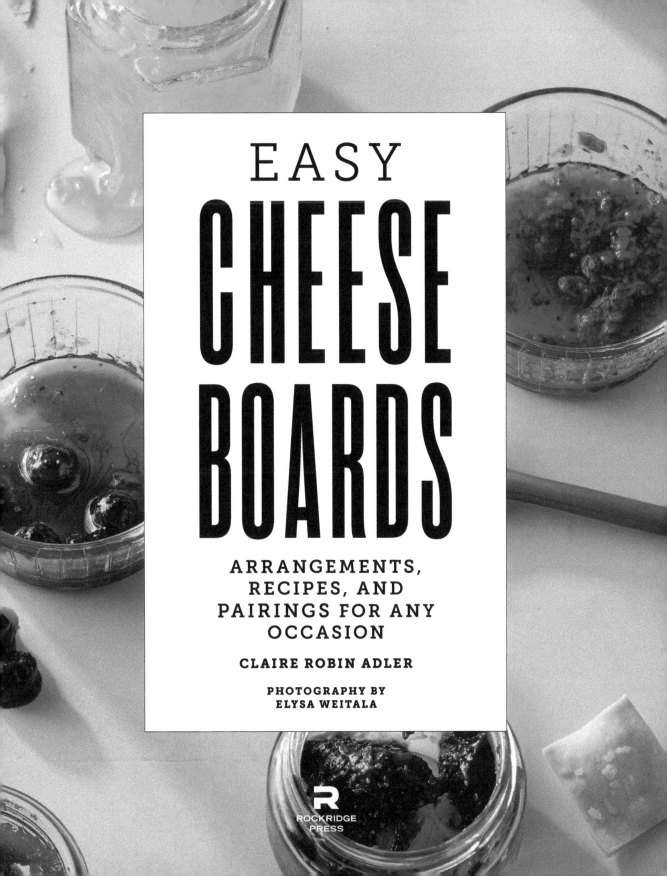

EASY CHEESE BOARDS

ARRANGEMENTS, RECIPES, AND PAIRINGS FOR ANY OCCASION

CLAIRE ROBIN ADLER

PHOTOGRAPHY BY ELYSA WEITALA

ROCKRIDGE PRESS

TO MY SISTER
KAREN ADLER,
WHO LOVES BOOKS
AND CHEESE.

CONTENTS

CHEESEMONGER'S WELCOME

I got started in the cheese industry for the same reason you probably picked up this book: I love cheese. I just wanted to eat good cheese and share it with others; I had no idea that I had walked into a world so rich in history, culture, and science. In my role as Cheese Director of a restaurant group, I learned to select the best cheeses and curate a menu of fantastic cheese boards. I learned to properly cut, plate, pair, and serve. I learned the stories behind each cheese I chose for any board: who made it, how it was made, and the history of each cheesemaker and cheese style. I taught classes to share these stories with restaurant staff and guests. Diners who walked in because they just really loved cheese walked away with a complete experience of stories, sensations, aromas, and flavors.

This world led me to explore the complexities of wine and beer and the principles of pairings. Knowing how to make a great cheese arrangement made me a better chef and host, and it will do the same for you. But if you simply want to make a cheese board because you just love cheese, then this book will show you how to do that, too. Either way, you're about to learn how to make beautiful cheese boards that taste as good as they look.

First and foremost, this book serves as a practical guide to putting a cheese board together. I'll walk you through every step of the process from imagining a plate to serving it. I will guide you through choosing the types of cheese, and then selecting them at the store. You'll learn to cut and plate cheese, prepare accompaniments, and present them all on an artful board. And when you're ready (and perhaps you're already there), this book will also give you the tools to add your own creativity and flair. You'll be able to tell the story behind different cheeses: how they were made, where they come from, and why they complete the ideal board. You'll learn that a great cheese board is more than a delicious appetizer, entertaining platter, or dessert: It's the careful curation of flavors and textures from different times and places, all of which contribute something unique to the board, the mood, and your senses.

You'll be surprised at how much fun it is to arrange a tantalizing cheese board and how something so easy to put together will wow at any occasion. Let's get started!

CHAPTER 1

INTRODUCTION TO CHEESE

THE LEGEND of cheesemaking says that a nomad, traveling across the desert, was carrying milk in a sack made from a sheep's stomach. After reaching his destination, he opened the sack to find his milk had separated into solids, and those solids—likely over 7,000 years ago—were the first cheese. Since then, cheesemaking has developed into both an art and a science.

MAKING AND AGING CHEESE

Cheesemaking starts with an animal—typically a cow, goat, or sheep—grazing on grass, clovers, herbs, or hay. The type of animal, breed, and its diet all affect the flavors of the milk it produces, and those flavor differences become even more pronounced in cheese, especially as it ages. Before even thinking about how to make cheese, the cheesemaker must consider where their milk comes from. Once the milk is chosen, the cheesemaker may choose to pasteurize it, which adds an extra layer of security to the cheesemaking process by killing certain bacteria.

Acid helps transform milk into cheese. In a few fresh cheeses, such as a basic home-made fromage blanc, the acids used include lemon juice or white vinegar. In nearly all cheeses, however, acidification is caused by starter cultures, or microbes, that help the fermentation process. While the milk ferments and acidifies, coagulation (the separation of solids from the liquids to form the curd) begins with the addition of a set of enzymes called rennet. Traditional rennet, also known as animal rennet, is extracted from the stomach of a calf, lamb, or goat kid, so cheeses made with traditional rennet are not strictly vegetarian. Traditional cheesemakers often prefer animal rennet for its coagulating properties and flavor profile—and certain European cheese recipes require it—but most widely distributed cheese is now made with a vegetarian rennet produced in a laboratory.

After the curds form, the cheesemaker cuts them. Smaller curds will create a drier cheese, which is best when making a cheese that's aged for a long time. A moisture rich, younger cheese will be made from curds cut into large pieces. The curds are then poured or ladled into molds that will form the final cheese's shape, and the curds are allowed to drain. The drained, protein-rich, and sweet liquid is called whey. Cheeses that will age for longer are also pressed to help expel more whey. The curds begin to knit together in this final form, and if the cheese will be aged, it is moved to a temperature- and humidity-controlled room: the cheese cave.

Most soft cheeses, such as ashy goat cheese and brie styles, are aged for somewhere between two and eight weeks, which gives the cheese enough time for a rind to begin to form. The rind forming process is caused by the cultures added at the beginning of acidification coming together and giving the cheese all its delicious flavor. Semi-firm cheeses, such as a younger manchego or tomme style, are usually aged for two to four months, and firmer cheeses are aged for anywhere from six months to years (few are aged for longer than two years). During the aging process, the cheesemaker, or *affineur* in French, will check on the cheeses to make sure they're aging properly. The affineur will taste the cheeses occasionally and rotate them so they age evenly. For certain cheese styles, they will pat the rinds down, brush them with a brine solution, or add other final ingredients such as herbs, flavors, and oils.

When the cheese is aged to perfection and ready for sale, it is transferred from the cheese cave to a refrigerator, where the much cooler temperatures greatly slow the speed of aging. Cheese is best eaten at room temperature in order to get all the flavors and aromas, so make sure that you store cheese in the refrigerator but take it out well before serving. The time it takes different cheeses to come to room temperature can vary, but 30 minutes to an hour is a good ballpark. Softer cheeses and smaller pieces will take around 30 minutes, whereas firmer cheeses or really large pieces will take closer to an hour.

TYPES OF CHEESE

Former president of France Charles de Gaulle famously said: "How can you govern a country that has two hundred and forty-six different kinds of cheese?" And that's just the types of *French* cheese— think of the hundreds more around the world. Cheesemongers generally divide cheese into five or six categories, based on how the cheeses are made. A cheese doesn't always fit neatly into one category, but a general understanding of the major cheese types will help you navigate any cheese counter or board.

FRESH CHEESE

Fresh cheese is, as the phrase might imply, cheese meant to be served soon after the

PASTEURIZED OR RAW?

Pasteurization is a heat treatment process that kills certain pathogens. In the United States, all cheeses that are aged for fewer than 60 days are legally required to be made with pasteurized milk, but in Europe, certain cheeses, such as Brie de Meaux, are required to be made with raw milk. Raw milk carries a higher risk of transmitting some bacteria, such as listeria, which is particularly dangerous for pregnant women or people with compromised immune systems. So, why not pasteurize all milk for cheesemaking? Cheese reflects the flavors from the animal's diet, the time of year the milk was produced, and even the land where the animal grazes. When milk is pasteurized, it's harder to retain those complex flavors specific to that batch. This book recommends both raw and pasteurized cheeses because both can be wonderful, but always consult a doctor before making decisions about your diet.

cheesemaking process. Besides its young age, fresh cheese is markedly different from any other cheese style because it is typically rindless and has a brighter white color; yellow and orange colors only develop with the aging process. Rinds take time to form, so a cheese that only spends a week or two—or sometimes less—in a cheese cave will not have a rind. Cheesemakers refer to a young cheese that will age as "green," and they call any cheese made to be eaten at that young age "fresh."

Some fresh cheeses, such as fromage blanc, can be served immediately after being made, but others, such as chèvre, might age anywhere from two to four weeks. Though slightly aged, chèvres are still considered to be part of the fresh cheese category because they're soft, spreadable, and rindless. The limited time in the cheese cave gives chèvre time to develop certain flavors and lose a small amount of moisture, but the cheese is still mild and creamy, often with a slight note of acidity or citrus.

Fresh cheeses are moisture rich and can sometimes even be made without rennet because they are meant to retain enough moisture so that the coagulating enzyme is unnecessary. This high moisture content makes fresh cheeses more prone to spoilage, as does the fact that they don't have rinds, which function to prevent bacteria entering the cheese.

Fresh cheese is also easy to make at home. All you need is milk (it can't be ultra-pasteurized, and whole milk works best) and an acid such as lemon juice (if you're okay with a little lemony flavor). With precise heating, timing, and addition of the acid, the milk will begin to separate into curds and whey, and when the process is complete, you can strain the whey from the curds with cheesecloth.

Because fresh cheese generally has a mild flavor, the pairing options are endless, but you'll want to be careful not to overwhelm the cheese. Fresh fruits and nuts are always a great option because the extra texture is welcome in a rich, creamy, spreadable fresh cheese.

FRESH CHEESES TO KNOW:
- **Chèvre (pasteurized goat; France):** tangy, hay, citric, zesty

- **Cottage cheese (pasteurized cow; Greece and the United States):** fresh curds dressed in cream and whey

- **Farmer's cheese (pasteurized cow, goat, or sheep; the United States and everywhere):** pressed, firmer than other fresh cheeses, mild, variable spreadability (depending on the farmer)

- **Fresh ricotta (pasteurized cow; Italy):** literally "recooked" whey, mild, creamy, fluffy, sweet

- **Fromage blanc (pasteurized cow; France and Belgium):** smooth, citric, lactic, mild

- **Mascarpone (pasteurized cow; Italy):** extra cream added, rich, buttery, filling

- **Queso fresco (pasteurized cow or goat; Mexico):** slightly tangy, clean, soft crumble

SOFT-RIPENED CHEESE

Soft-ripened cheese covers a diverse range of cheeses because it includes any cheese that has been . . . well, ripened to be soft. Cheesemongers further divide soft-ripened cheese into two subcategories: bloomy rind and washed rind.

Note that most soft-ripened cheeses last only about two weeks in the refrigerator because of their high moisture content. Softer cheeses generally have a shorter shelf life, whereas a firmer bloomy or washed rind cheese may last longer. Soft cheeses should be served at room temperature, as any other cheese. However, although firmer cheeses can spend hours out of the refrigerator, for food safety reasons, softer cheeses should not be left out for more than four hours.

BLOOMY RIND

The term, "bloomy rind," comes from the appearance of the cheese rind as it ages and forms. Under a microscope, the rind looks like it's made of tiny blooming flowers, which, to the naked eye, forms the fuzzy white rind we know and love. The blooming molds ripen the cheese from the outside in, breaking down proteins, softening the cheese, and imparting aromas that are often earthy, mushroomy, and garlicky. Some bloomy rinds are mild, buttery, creamy, and even sweet with just a touch of earthiness, whereas others can smell of roasted cauliflower, dirt, straw, and onion. Take note of this with your drink pairings and choose delicate bubbles to cut through rich and buttery brie styles. Many brie-style cheeses are double-crèmes, which are bloomy rinds with extra cream added to the milk to give the cheese a bit more richness. A triple-crème is a bloomy rind that has so much added cream the cheese ends up being about 75 percent fat by dry matter. These cheeses are extra luscious, silky, and crazily decadent. Pair earthy but light-bodied red wines with more pungent styles of bloomy rind cheese, such as a French Burgundy with Délice de Bourgogne.

Some bloomy rinds have a wrinkly rind and look almost like a brain. Wrinkly cheeses are mostly made from goat milk, and the wrinkling comes from a yeast that creates the brainy appearance and imparts the musty, yeasty, and fermented flavors. Some wrinkly rind goat cheeses are coated in a dark black vegetable ash. Cheesemaking long predates modern refrigeration, and as a result, many cheese styles focus on how to make the cheese last. Coating a cheese in burnt vegetable scraps, vegetable ash, or even storing it in an ash-filled box helps keep away bugs and bacteria. Today, with refrigeration and other food safety measures, using vegetable ash has more to do with appearance, flavor, and tradition than it does with an extended shelf life.

ASH CHEESES TO KNOW:

- **Sainte Maure (raw goat; France):** shaped like a small log, citric, slightly peppery, tangy

- **Valençay (raw goat; France):** shaped like a truncated pyramid, grassy, black pepper, lemon

OTHER BLOOMY RINDS TO KNOW:

- **Brie de Meaux (raw cow; France):** sweet, buttery, mushroom, truffles, salt, cream

- **Brillat-Savarin (pasteurized cow; France):** triple-crème, pillowy, soft, rich, decadent, nuts, truffles

- **Camembert de Normandie (raw cow; France):** hay, truffles, garlic, fruity, woodsy

- **Cowgirl Creamery Mt. Tam (pasteurized cow; United States):** firmer triple-crème, milky, white mushrooms, cultured butter, grass

- **Vermont Creamery Cremont (pasteurized cow and goat; United States):** luxurious texture, creamy, mouth-coating

WASHED RIND

Washed rind cheeses, also known as stinky cheeses, are made in a similar way to a bloomy rind, making them soft and moisture rich. They are also literally washed; cheesemakers carefully create a brine solution with which they regularly and evenly brush the cheese. The washing creates the right environment to grow certain bacteria that impart funky flavors and aromas. The smell of stinky cheese can be intense and reminiscent of barnyards, hay, rusticity, and wet basements. These aromas are, admittedly, not for everyone, but the smell tends to be stronger than the taste of the cheese, so give it a try. The same bacteria that make a cheese pungent can also make it smell fruity, and the right drink pairing, such as a honeyed riesling or sweet dessert wine, can bring out delicious fruit flavors.

Not all washed rind cheeses are soft. Any cheese can be washed, and other styles generally are, such as tommes, a semisoft style, and alpines, a harder style, both traditionally made in the Alps of France, Italy, Germany, and Switzerland. Although these cheeses are technically washed rind, they are more frequently referred to specifically as tommes or Alpines and differ in flavor and texture. Washed rinds have a beautiful color rind that ranges from coral to orange to red to brown, so don't be alarmed if you see a smattering of colors and molds growing.

WASHED RIND CHEESES TO KNOW:

- **Cowgirl Creamery Red Hawk (pasteurized cow; United States):** triple-crème and washed, beefy, salty, rich

- **Époisses (raw or pasteurized cow; France):** washed in brandy, extra pungent, brothy, bacony, silky

- **Stinking Bishop (pasteurized cow; England):** washed in perry (pear cider), pungent, savory, meaty

- **Taleggio (pasteurized cow; Italy):** fruity, tangy, salty, meaty

HARD CHEESE

Hard cheeses have firmer textures and less moisture, meaning that they have a longer shelf life. The firmer and drier the cheese, the longer it will keep in and out of the refrigerator. Harder cheeses can be further divided into the following helpful styles.

SEMI-FIRM CHEESE

Designated as uncooked pressed cheeses, semi-firm cheeses vary in texture, color, and flavor. Many cheeses that are not soft-ripened are still fairly pliable because the curds aren't cut that small during the cheesemaking process and they're aged for only two to four months to preserve a slightly soft texture. They are pressed during the cheesemaking process to help them firm up.

PRESSED CHEESES TO KNOW:

- **Manchego (pasteurized sheep; Spain):** rustic, buttery, oily, wooly

- **Tomme, toma (raw cow; France and Italy):** minerally, musty, vegetal, fruit, often with holes, like soft and small Alpine

FIRM CHEESES (COOKED PRESSED CHEESES)

Firm cheeses, or cooked pressed cheeses, can be aged between a few months and several years, and as they age, the flavors usually become more intense. If you want your cheese to age for a long time, it's important to remove more moisture. Bad bacteria can grow in moisture rich cheeses during the aging process, so firmer, more aged cheeses go through an extra process of cooking the curds before they're formed into molds to help expel moisture. Cooking the curds releases their natural sugars, which often gives cooked curd cheeses their nutty, brothy, sweet, caramelly notes and flavors.

Alpine cheese (what cheesemakers call swiss cheese), cheddar, gouda, pecorino, and Parmigiano-Reggiano are some of the most widely known cooked pressed cheeses.

ALPINE CHEESES TO KNOW:

- **Appenzeller (raw cow; Switzerland):** floral, roasted nuts, fruity, herbal, grassy

- **Comté (raw cow; France):** cooked milk, dried fruit, almond

- **Emmenthaler (raw cow; Switzerland):** buttery, fruity, sharp, meltable, large holes

- **Gruyère (raw cow; Switzerland):** brothy, brown butter, hazelnut

CHEDDAR CHEESES TO KNOW:
- **Cabot Clothbound Cheddar (pasteurized cow; United States):** nutty, savory, tangy, sweet caramel

- **Grafton Cheddar (pasteurized or raw cow; United States):** zippy, sweet cream, hay, cultured milk

- **Quicke's Clothbound Cheddar (pasteurized cow; England):** horseradish, butter, apples

GOUDA CHEESES TO KNOW:
- **Beemster (pasteurized cow; Holland):** dense, caramel, sweet, creamy

- **Ewephoria (pasteurized sheep; Holland):** extra sweet, butterscotch, nutty

- **Roomano (pasteurized cow; Holland):** lower fat take on gouda, salty and sweet, toffee, dense

PECORINO AND PARMESAN CHEESES TO KNOW:
- **Parmesan (pasteurized cow; everywhere):** take on the real deal that's slightly milder but still salty and savory

- **Parmigiano-Reggiano (raw cow; Italy):** complex, savory, salty, fruity, gritty, crumbly

- **Pecorino Romano (pasteurized or raw sheep; Italy):** intense salt, piquant, oily, granular

- **Pecorino Toscano (pasteurized or raw sheep; Italy):** oily, salty, buttery, savory and sweet, mild pepper, nutty

BLUE CHEESE

When you think of blue cheese, you may have an immediate reaction: *ick!* or *yum!* Whatever your opinion might be, you might be surprised by the wide variety of blue cheeses. Though all blue cheeses have some of that bluish-greenish hue sprinkled throughout, the flavors range from intense, spicy, and pungent to rich, creamy, and fudgy, and textures range from crumbly with crystals to smooth and spreadable.

There are a few peculiarities to the characteristic mold—and yes, it is mold—that makes blue cheese blue. The mold grows only when it's exposed to oxygen, so blue cheese is pierced with needles to let air into the center of the cheese. You can often see blue veins running along a straight line or holes on the outside of the cheese wheel, which tell you where the cheese was pierced. As you may expect, these blue veins make the cheese spicy, peppery, and piquant, but they also impart the cheese with fruity, citric, and chocolatey flavors. You may have heard that the mold is penicillin or that those with penicillin allergies should stay away from blue cheese. Not true! The two kinds of blue mold have similar names, *Penicillium roqueforti* and *Penicillium glaucum*, but they're only distant cousins of the penicillin medicine. So, please indulge.

The blue veins also only grow where there's lots of salt, so blue cheese is usually quite salty, making it the ideal cheese to pair with something sweet, such as chocolate, figs, or a dessert wine. Not only does blue cheese pair perfectly with romantic offerings like dark chocolate covered cherries, but it also has a romantic discovery story.

Blue cheese was a happy accident discovered in the Middle Ages in Italy. The legend goes that a young cheesemaker's apprentice became distracted by his lover while he was making a batch of cheese and ran off to spend time with her. When he came back a week later, he found that his batch had blue veins running through it. Instead of throwing it away, he tried it and found that his cheese had added complexity; it was spicy and peppery with fruity sweetness.

This was the birth of gorgonzola, one of the most famous blue cheeses in the world.

BLUES TO KNOW:
- **Cabrales (raw cow, goat, and sheep; Spain):** spicy, salty, sharp, pungent, herbal

- **Danish Blue (pasteurized cow; Denmark):** crumbly, white peppercorns, buttery

- **Gorgonzola (pasteurized cow; Italy):** decadent, chocolate, figs, black pepper

- **Great Hill Blue (raw cow; Massachusetts, United States):** bright, zippy, light pepper, crumbly

- **Point Reyes Original Blue (raw cow; California, United States):** sweet fruit, medium blue punch, tang

- **Roquefort (raw sheep; France):** peppery, juicy, citric, piquant

- **Stilton (pasteurized cow; England):** fudgy, creamy, hay, nutty, smooth

VEGAN CHEESE

Vegan cheese is not dairy, and it is very different in flavor, texture, and, of course, process from dairy cheese. But it can still be delicious. Vegan cheese is a great addition to any cheese board, either to provide variety in flavors and options, or to serve primarily as a dairy alternative if you or your guests follow a plant-based diet. Much like vegan milks, vegan cheeses are usually made from nuts or soy but can be made from other ingredients such as seeds, grains, and oils.

Because this book focuses on cheese board arrangements, we'll be discussing vegan cheeses that can stand alone on a board and also pair well with the delicious accompaniments and beverages throughout this guide. Daiya Foods is probably the best known vegan cheese producer in the United States. The company has been making vegan cheeses since the 1980s, but Daiya's products are generally geared toward providing dairy alternatives for dishes like mac 'n' "cheese," burritos, pizzas, and baked goods.

Vegan cheesemakers often use the same microbes and cultures that dairy cheese-makers use, resulting in similarly earthy or creamy flavors. The fermentation process gives both dairy and vegan options real acidity, which is often perceived as a tangy or sharp flavor. Although vegan cheese might be creamy, it will not have the same lactic notes from the animal's diet. And, of course, a nut cheese will be nutty and fatty, whereas a soy based cheese might have flavors reminiscent of miso.

Vegan-friendly grocers may stock an option or two, but vegan cheese can be difficult to find, so when in doubt, try ordering online or even making a recipe at home.

VEGAN CHEESES TO KNOW:

- **Bute Island Blue French Style Sheese (coconut oil and starch)**: peppery spice, pleasant bitterness

- **Dr-Cow Aged Macadamia Cheese (macadamia nut)**: sweet, nutty, firm

- **Miyoko's Black Ash (cashews and miso)**: buttery, sweet, mild tang, dense

- **Miyoko's Sharp Farmhouse (cashews and miso)**: tangy, sharp, fruity, rustic, firm but melty, salty

- **Treeline Classic Aged Nut Cheese (cashews)**: smoky, mild, creamy

- **Violife Just Like Parmesan (coconut oil and starch)**: savory, nutty, shreddable

- **Vromage Brie-Truffle (mixed nuts and seeds)**: earthy, mushroomy, creamy, rich, spreadable

CHEESE AROUND THE WORLD

The United States has primarily adapted the extensively codified cheesemaking tradition from Western Europe, and, for the most part, this book focuses on styles that originate from that part of the world. Because of its long history of cheesemaking, Europe has regulated about 200 cheeses by giving them *name protection*. Name protection means that you're not allowed to make camembert outside of Normandy, France, or if you do, you can't call it by its full name, Camembert de Normandie. Other name protected cheeses include Roquefort in France, Asiago in Italy, and Queso Manchego in Spain. Name protections include more than the area of production and often include the breed of the milked animal, whether the milk must be raw or pasteurized, the temperatures at different points in the process, and more. So why do we see these names used in the United States? First, only the specific name is protected (e.g., Parmigiano-Reggiano is protected, parmesan is not). And second, not all protections extend outside of Europe. You can make any style of cheese anywhere, and it will taste much the same if you use high quality ingredients and know your stuff. But it won't have the terroir from that specific place.

There are also wonderful cheeses from India, Ethiopia, Brazil—pretty much anywhere that there are dairy animals. For the most part, traditional cheeses from Africa, South America, and Asia are primarily used as an ingredient in cooking rather than a feature on a cheese board. But that's not to say they don't have a space. Mild queso fresco and Oaxaca cheese are not too difficult to find and can be served on a board with some regional pairings, like a pineapple-jalapeño jelly or pickled cactus. Indian paneer is probably best for a savory meal, but it could be adventurous to try it on a board served with a sweet and sour mango chutney.

CHAPTER 2

BUILDING YOUR CHEESE BOARD

PUTTING TOGETHER a cheese board may seem daunting because there are so many options for each element. Remember that it's a *cheese* board, first and foremost, meaning that if you feature cheese that you like, all the other elements will follow. Not every component needs to be on every cheese board: Add the elements that complement your chosen cheeses' flavors, textures, aromas, and stories, and your cheeses' complexities and wonders will shine.

Putting together a cheese board is about understanding composition, or how the components come together to make a whole that is greater than the sum of its parts. This means understanding the textures, flavors, and aromas of each component. It also means understanding the art of pairing. This chapter will walk you through the basics of each component and how they come together in flavors and presentation.

Part of the art of cheese board curation is thinking about the purpose of your board. Are you serving a pre-dinner course, entertaining for a party, or closing out a meal? You'll find appetizer boards in chapter 3, platters for entertaining in chapter 4, and dessert cheese boards in chapter 5. Most of the arrangements will have at least one element that you can prepare at home, and all the recipes for those will be found in chapter 6 (for dips, spreads, and jams) and chapter 7 (for other sorts of flavorful accompaniments).

ESTABLISHING A FLAVOR PROFILE

Understanding the five basic tastes—sweet, salty, sour, bitter, and umami—is essential to learning how to create and balance flavor. *Sweet* and *salty* are straightforward: We've all had sugar and salt. You know you're tasting something *sour* or acidic because your mouth may pucker a little or salivate in response to the tartness—think of lemons or pickle juice. *Bitterness* can be a bit harder to identify because, on its own, it can be unpleasant, such as dark roast black coffee or unsweetened cocoa, but, when combined with other flavors, it can provide needed balance and complexity. The fifth taste, *umami*, is a savory flavor that can be identified in mushrooms, beef bouillon, and soy sauce. Often mistaken for saltiness (because they go so well together), umami is distinct, providing deep, rich, savory flavors. Umami plays a particularly important role in aged cheeses because proteins break down into amino acids that are high in umami flavors (parmesan is a classic example). Understanding and identifying these five basic flavors is crucial to creating a balanced cheese board where accompaniments are used to highlight rather than overwhelm the flavors.

Just as important as flavor is aroma. Your nose perceives more than your tongue, and although you can technically only distinguish five flavors on your tongue, your nose provides all the extra nuance. Always be sure to smell your cheese as well as taste it! When smelling cheese, there's no right or wrong; what you smell is what there is. Someone might think that a hunk of cheddar smells like leather, and someone else might say that it smells like an apple orchard. You're both right, and that's where the creativity and fun come in.

PRIMARY CHEESE FLAVORS

Cheese is diverse, and, as you learned in chapter 1, there are so many different kinds that all taste and smell unique. But at the end of the day, all cheese is fermented milk, and it all has certain flavors in different proportions. All cheese is at least slightly acidic because lactic acid is produced by fermentation. The term "sharp" usually refers to a cheese's acidity level, but other words used to describe a cheese's acidity include tangy, sour, or piquant.

All cheeses contain varying degrees of salt. Blue cheese is made with a lot of salt in order to create the right conditions for the blue mold to grow, and aged hard cheeses are often a bit saltier because high salt levels help the cheese remove moisture and, therefore, last longer.

Milk naturally contains sugar, so many cheeses have a natural sweetness. Some aromas—fruitiness and caramelization, for example—are often perceived as sweetness, and that's just as important as sugary sweetness.

Other cheeses reflect the animal it comes from. Goat cheese tends to be grassy, citric, and peppery. Sheep cheese tends to be oily, buttery, nutty, and, well, wooly. Cow cheese might be the most varied in flavor, but it's often earthy, herbaceous, and even beefy.

PRIMARY CHEESE TEXTURES

Cheese, like fruit, has a point at which it is ripe, so it follows that a cheese can be either under- or overripe. For a soft cheese, overripe cheese can become so gooey in the middle that it's almost like soup. The flavor may also become off-putting, with a strong smell of ammonia. For a hard cheese, overripeness is usually identifiable as a dried out texture as opposed to a pleasant crumbliness.

Of course, just like taste, enjoyment of texture is subjective. Some people love a super ripe brie that practically oozes when cut, and others prefer a cheese with a little more structure. A cheesemonger might have one preference, but yours might be different, so seek out your preferred textures just as you do flavors.

Certain aged cheeses, like goudas and Alpines, often have little crunchy bits that are pleasantly studded throughout a smooth cheese. These are called tyrosine crystals and are formed as a cheese matures. Other well-aged cheeses, such as Parmigiano-Reggiano, can give your mouth a bit of a tingly feeling. Some find this unpleasant, even a bit itchy, but it's often just a slight zing. Cheeses that are itchier are sometimes best saved for grating over pasta or other recipes and better left off a cheese board unless paired carefully with an acidic or starchy accompaniment.

Textures are fun to play with when it comes to drink pairings and are typically an opportunity to show some contrast. Got a really rich, buttery cheese? Pair it with fine bubbles or a lot of acidity to cut through the fat. Got a crumbly cheddar? Pair it with a silky-smooth chardonnay.

REGIONAL FLAVORS

Much like wine, cheese can reflect the place in which it is made. This concept is called *terroir*, a French word with no exact English translation that refers to the region or subregion, time of year, weather, soils, and even the foliage of the place where a cheese or wine is from.

Terroir, however, is not unique to European produced cheeses; every place contributes to a cheese's flavors and aromas. The weather, seasons, and soils affect what grows, which affects an animal's diet, and that changes the composition of the milk the animal produces. This means that a cheese made in the exact same way but from two different herds in different parts of the world will taste different. Try cheeses local to your region and see how they differ in taste from imported cheese or those from the opposite side of the country.

Different regions lead to a variety of flavors because of varied cheesemaking traditions across the world. French cheeses are often complex, sometimes funky, musty, and yeasty. Italy is known for cheeses that are great to grate, meaning savory, salty, and well-aged. Spain is home to many goats and sheep and many mixed-milk cheeses, which are often nutty, buttery, and piquant. Although the United States might be known for making primarily processed cheeses, American artisan cheese producers follow European cheesemaking traditions, oftentimes transforming European flavors for an American palate, which usually means lots of salt and milder flavors.

Knowing the region where a cheese is made won't always tell you exactly what it will taste like, but it can help with pairings. When in doubt, follow the tenet of chefs and sommeliers: What grows together, goes together.

SEASONAL CHEESE AND PRODUCE

We all know that fruits and vegetables are seasonal, so it's no surprise that cheese is, too. Eating fresh fruits and vegetables that are in season is not only the best way to get the most flavor out of your food, but it's also a great way to appreciate the time of year, weather, and the current season. A great thing about the seasonality of food is that it tends to match up with what you'd naturally want to eat at that time of year.

For example, goat's milk cheeses tend to be most available during spring and summer because of the milking season. Bright and grassy, fresh chèvres pair well with highly acidic fruits and vegetables, such as citrus, watermelon, and beets, all of which are available over the summer months (see Summer Freshness on page 51).

Winter calls for warming spices and toasted nuts, and although it can be harder to find fresh produce, winter is a great time to enjoy pickled products preserved from warmer months. Cheeses made in the winter tend to be richer and fattier due to the animal's sparser winter diet. This richness helps you stay warm in winter, but these cheeses could benefit from pairing with something that can cut through their fatty goodness (see Winter Warmth on page 49).

Fall fruits, such as apples and pears, bring out the natural sweet and fruity flavors in many cheeses. So, in the fall, an arrangement with cheddars and blues that have pear- and apple-like aromas is delightful (see Fall Flavors on page 46).

Spring brings new life and flowers, so opt for a floral or herbaceous cheese, such as a tomme or Manchego, or even a cheese coated in flowers, like Alp Blossom or Hudson Flower, if you're able to find those at a specialty cheese shop (see Springtime Bloom on page 47).

SPECIAL OCCASIONS AND HOLIDAYS

There's a cheese for every holiday or occasion. In general, celebrations call for something bubbly to drink, so you can't go wrong with luscious cheeses. Try double- and triple-crèmes such as Fromager d'Affinois or Délice de Bourgogne. But really, any brie style will do because its fatty richness will make you crave bubbles,

ACHIEVING THE PERFECT PAIRING

Creating the perfect pairing is all about complementing flavors and balance. Sometimes, you want a contrast. A classic delicious flavor contrast is sweet and salty—think dessert wine and blue cheese. At other times, pairing like with like is the way to go; acidity generally goes well with more acidity, such as a tangy goat cheese with an acidic sauvignon blanc. Bitterness can be unpleasant in large quantities, so avoid pairing a bitter cheese with a bitter wine or beer. For example, brie styles can have a pleasant, mild bitterness, especially on the rind, but it's usually off-putting when consumed with a bitter IPA or a tannic red wine.

In addition to flavor, it's important to think about intensity of taste. A mild, fresh cheese might go well with a light-bodied, spritzy white wine, such as vinho verde, but it would be totally overwhelmed by an oaky chardonnay. Similarly, a strong and spicy blue cheese, such as Roquefort, would drown out the complex flavors of a light-bodied, fruity pinot noir.

The examples we've discussed so far have been about drink pairings, but accompaniments to cheese should be considered in the same way. Because all cheese is at least a little salty, many classic accompaniments are sweet, such as fruits and jams. Honey is often the go-to accompaniment because it's sweet but also has a lot of acidity, which naturally goes with the tanginess of cheese. Here are a few more pairing go-tos:

- Fresh goat cheese and sauvignon blanc (paired high acid notes)
- Stinky cheese and riesling (salty and sweet)
- Brie and bubbly (fatty and fine textured)
- Cheddar and amber or brown ale (paired brown butter notes)
- Gouda and whiskey (paired caramelized flavors; whiskey strength cuts gouda fat)
- Blue cheese and dessert wine, such as port (salty and sweet)

These principles are helpful, but if you really want to be sure you've made a great pairing, taste your two (or more) elements together. The most important thing is that you like it!

and those tiny bubbles cut through fat, allowing you to keep enjoying copious amounts of decadent goodness (see Decadence and Bubbles on page 52).

Most holidays have an established flavor profile, so creating the best cheese board for that day means thinking about what else you'll be eating and sharing, and picking cheeses that fit the vibe. Chocolate for Valentine's Day? Try a salty blue that pairs well with dark chocolate and strawberries (see Chocolate and Cheese on page 68). Cranberry sauce at Thanksgiving? Find a sweet and crunchy gouda that will balance with the smooth texture and tartness of the berries. Grilling for Independence Day? Try a smoked cheddar and meaty stinky cheese to eat with your roast.

Holidays are special times, so when in doubt, ask what's new and exciting at your local cheese shop or specialty aisle in the grocery store. The cheese doesn't need to be perfectly matched to the day, but sometimes, picking a cheese from a local, one-off batch that you might not be able to get anywhere else is the best way to commemorate a special day.

HOW TO CUT CHEESE

Although you want to be sure your cheese is not too cold when you serve it, you don't want to cut it until right before it will be served (if you're going to cut it at all). Soft cheeses are easy for your guests to cut themselves, as are some crumbly cheeses. But a cheese's flavor will last longest if you don't cut into it, so don't feel like you have to cut everything in advance. Plus, the less you pre-cut, the more you can save the leftovers for yourself (if you have any).

If you do cut into a cheese, be sure to retain its general shape. For example, if you have a small wheel, cut it like a pie to keep its circular shape. If you have a triangular wedge, don't cut off the tip (known as the nose), but cut along the long side of the triangle to maintain its triangular shape. Not only does it look more beautiful to keep the cheese's shape, but each slice also evenly distributes the rind and the interior of the cheese, which often have very different tastes and textures. Triangles are aesthetically pleasing and come in many different forms (think back to math class!), so even if you cut all your cheeses into triangles, you can still have a lot of variation. Avoid cutting square and rectangular pieces, which are reminiscent of those prepackaged cheese boards someone picks up for an office party. If you have a block of cheese that's more naturally cut into rectangles or squares, just halve the rectangles diagonally to make triangles. Long sticks are also a nice shape for cheese (like halved celery sticks) if you want to expand beyond triangles.

It's best to serve a cheese with at least some of its rind. Although not everyone enjoys eating the rind, all cheese rinds are edible unless a clearly inedible substance has been added to the exterior of the cheese, such as wax, cloth, paper, or bark. Serving cheese with its rind is more beautiful and allows everyone the option of tasting the rind; sometimes, the best flavor is hidden just beneath the rind.

You might have some leftover cheese scraps after trimming the cheese into even shapes. There are many uses for these, including *fromage fort*, a strong French cheese spread invented for exactly this reason. You can make fromage fort at home (see below). You can also use cheese scraps in salads or melted on chips, toast, or vegetables.

CHEESE EQUIPMENT

You don't need anything fancy to prepare a cheese board, but there are a few tools that can make your life a lot easier. If possible, try to serve each cheese with a separate tool. Pre-cut cheeses can be served with toothpicks or as finger foods, but if you're serving a whole wedge or wheel, it's best to have a separate tool for each cheese to avoid mixing the flavors. No one expects their brie to taste like blue cheese.

FROMAGE FORT

It's amazingly easy to turn your cheese scraps into a delicious spread, which you can smear on crusty baguettes or crackers, or simply melt on toast. You can collect any type of cheese scraps—soft, hard, or blue—and keep them in the refrigerator until you have enough to make some spread. You probably want at least half a pound of cheese, but the recipe is extremely flexible.

To make the spread, coarsely chop the soft cheeses and grate the hard cheeses. Remove and discard any hard rinds and moldy patches. Put all the cheese in a food processor with about three tablespoons of dry white wine and one garlic clove per half pound of cheese, adding more as needed to process. If you have more hard cheese than soft, add a few pats of butter. You can also substitute vegetable broth for some or all of the white wine, if desired. Process the cheese mixture until it's soft and creamy but not quite smooth. Add salt and pepper to taste (and definitely taste because salt is not always needed), and garnish it with parsley or chives. Use it immediately or store it for a few days in a tightly packed crock in the refrigerator, and the flavors will grow stronger (the "*fort*" in fromage fort means strong). Let the spread warm up to room temperature before you serve it, or broil it for a few minutes and serve it as a dip.

- **Cheese Wire:** A cheese wire is a metal wire strung between two handles, allowing you to cut through soft cheeses cleanly and precisely. Cheese wires are especially helpful with fresh cheeses, letting you cut them without smooshing them. If you don't have a cheese wire, unflavored dental floss works, too.

- **Soft-Cheese Knife:** Soft cheese loses its shape easily and sticks to knives. A soft-cheese knife, also known as a brie knife, either has a very thin blade or has large holes in it so there is less surface area on the knife that the cheese comes into contact with.

- **Fork-Tipped Knife:** This knife allows you to cut hard cheeses normally or use the forked tip to crumble the cheese. Some aged cheeses, such as clothbound cheddar, are hard to cut cleanly and can look beautiful if you crumble them into bite-size pieces.

- **Ramekins:** Small ramekins are one of the most helpful tools on a board. Ramekins, or individual small bowls, are traditionally used for small baked goods and are perfect for serving condiments, such as honeys, jams, and olives. Although cheeses are meant to be tasted with their accompaniments, it's best to keep spreads separated from cheeses on the board, allowing you and your guests to choose whether to eat two particular components together. Plus, honey in a

ramekin is much easier to clean up than honey on a board. If you don't own many small ramekins, get creative: Espresso cups, tiny jars, and small dishes meant for salts and dips are great alternatives and add variety to your board.

THE SIX ELEMENTS OF A BOARD

Breaking down a cheese board into its six main elements makes the board a little easier to compose. The cheese is obviously the focal point, but every element plays an important role, although on each cheese board that role might be slightly different. When thinking about all of the non-cheese elements on the board, always consider pairings and place each item closest to the cheese you think it pairs with best.

Every cheese board needs something sweet, something salty, something acidic, something smooth, and something crunchy. But your smooth and crunchy elements can double as your acidic, salty, or sweet components. Fruits and fruit-based spreads are both sweet and acidic, whereas pickles and olives are both salty and acidic. If you're a vegetarian and want to leave charcuterie off the board, no problem; just make sure you've included something else in that salty spot. Salted nuts are a great alternative and are hearty like meat, but you can get creative: chips, popcorn, olives, and sardines (for the pescatarians) are all less classic but awesomely interesting salty elements.

As long as you have these flavors and textures, you can present a thoughtful, well-rounded board. A good starting place is to pick one from each of these six elements: cheese; charcuterie; produce; dips, spreads, and jams; other accompaniments; and bread and crackers. I've also included an optional seventh element for adding some extra flair to your board.

CHEESE

Pick your cheeses first, and then plan the other elements to complement them. Your choices might be influenced by the wines you have at home or the jam someone gifted you, but the cheese is ultimately the star of the cheese board, and picking your cheeses for balance, harmony, and variety is a great way to start.

If you don't know how many cheeses to pick, use the rule of three. Three cheeses provide room for very different types of cheese without overwhelming the board. Two cheeses can make for a nice appetizer or dessert for just a couple of people, but one cheese hardly counts as a cheese board unless it's a very special cheese or you transform it in some way, such as making Baked Brie with Wine-Poached Cherries (page 32). The more people you have, the more cheeses you can reasonably get away

with, but anything more than six starts to become daunting. Estimate for 1 to 1.5 ounces of each cheese per person so that everyone gets to taste each cheese. Aim on the lighter side if you have more of each cheese or if you're serving it along with a lot of other foods. Plan for more of each if you have fewer cheeses or if the cheese is the star of your meal, party, or day. The cheese boards in this book follow these guidelines.

CHARCUTERIE

Charcuterie, or cured meats, are a wonderful addition to any cheese board. Charcuterie (known as *salumi* in Italian—not to be confused with salami, which is a type of salumi) is the French word that encompasses cured and smoked meats. Most charcuterie is fermented, so, like cheese, it has funky, musty, and tangy qualities. Of course, charcuterie is savory (lots of umami flavor) and salty, making it a great element to bring out those similar flavors in your cheese.

There are several types of charcuterie to know, and all can have a role to play on your cheese board.

- **Whole-muscle cuts** are cured meats that are packed with salt and spices and aged for anywhere from four weeks to a couple of years. Some whole-muscle cuts are also cold smoked after they're aged. Whole-muscle cuts are thinly sliced to be served as charcuterie or can be sliced

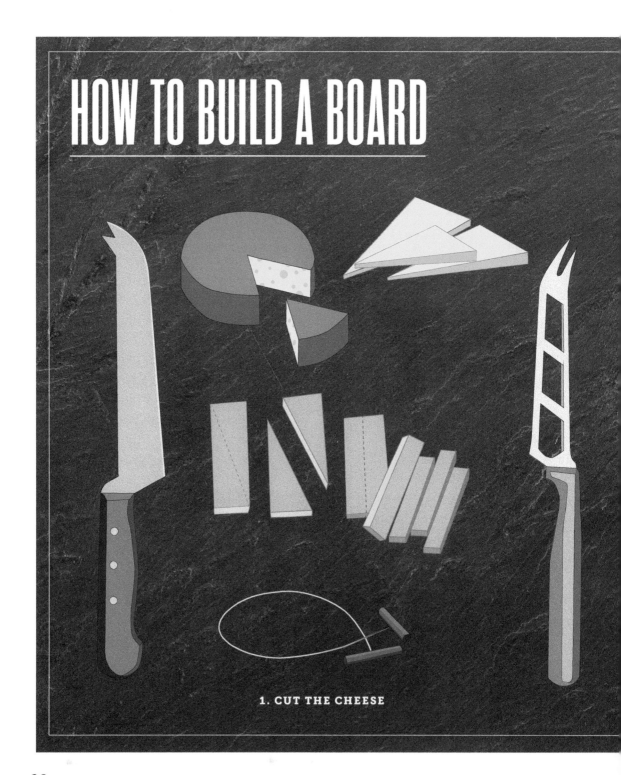

HOW TO BUILD A BOARD

1. CUT THE CHEESE

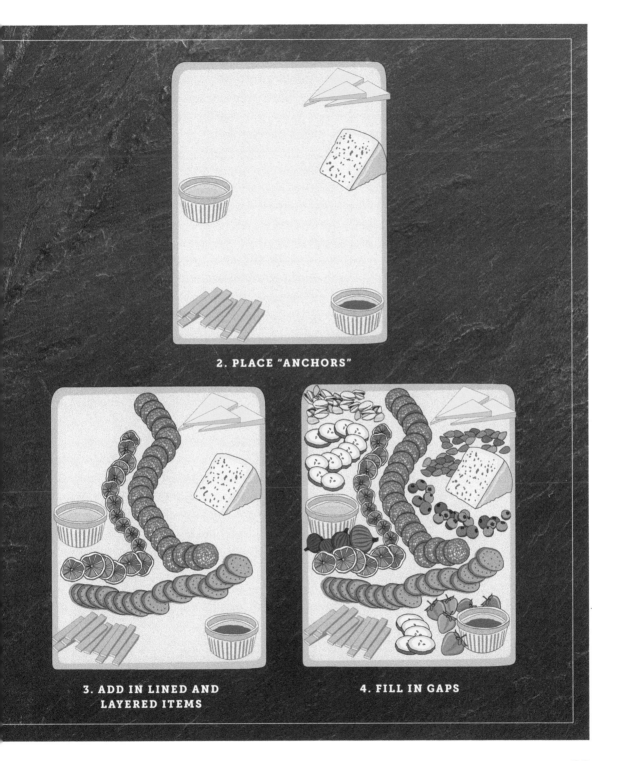

2. PLACE "ANCHORS"

3. ADD IN LINED AND
LAYERED ITEMS

4. FILL IN GAPS

thicker to enjoy in a sandwich. Most well-known whole-muscle meats are pork, including prosciutto (cut from the hind leg), coppa (cut from the collar), lonza (cut from the loin), and jamón ibérico (Spanish for fatty leg). Bresaola is a whole-muscle cured meat usually made from beef, and lamb and duck prosciuttos are also worth trying.

- **Cured sausages** are also cured in salt and spices to be aged and dried, but they differ from whole-muscle meats in that they're made from chopped or ground meat. They can also incorporate spices, herbs, and dried berries. Some well-known cured sausages include saucisson sec (the classic French sausage with garlic and black peppercorns), soppressata (extra-fatty, coarsely ground Italian sausage), chorizo (spicy, garlicky, coarsely ground sausage from Spain), and finocchiona (Italian sausage from the shoulder and spiced with fennel).

- **Terrine, pâté, rillettes, and mousse** are softer charcuterie options. Terrine is ground meat (or even seafood) that is bound together with boiled eggs and often blended with vegetables and herbs, and then formed in a loaf shape mold and served in bread shape slices. Terrine sometimes is served in a pastry crust or with a jelly topping. Pâté is the most similar to terrine; some people use the terms interchangeably, but pâté is

typically made mostly or entirely from the liver and can be served in any shape. Rillettes are cooked and shredded meats, fish, or poultry that are preserved in fat (often its own) and spreadable. Mousses are usually made from liver and incorporate cream or butter to give them a light, fluffy, and creamy texture.

PRODUCE

Fresh fruits bring sweetness, crisp acidity, and seasonality to your board.

Because cheese is salty, sweeter fruits are safe choices. Dried fruits, such as figs, apricots, and cherries, are sweeter than their fresh counterparts, although fresh berries often have a nice balance of sweetness and acidity that work well with younger, fresher cheeses. Although acidity in fruit can be great, don't go overboard: citrus fruits, such as oranges, grapefruits, and kiwis, are going to make your cheese seem unpleasantly curdled. Citrus flavors are great, but it's best to serve them as candies or preserves.

Grapes are perhaps the most common fresh fruit that is served with cheese. Grapes can be tricky, however, because their skins are tannic (just like wine), and tannins add astringency, which can bring out unpleasantness in the more naturally bitter cheeses. Be sure to pair grapes carefully.

The classic crudité board with raw carrots, celery, broccoli, cucumbers, and the like doesn't work as well on a cheese board; although, texturally, the vegetables might be great for hummus or a ranch dip, they don't work the same way with cheese. In addition, the sugars and flavors that make vegetables delicious taste much better with cheese when they've been roasted, pickled, or otherwise cooked. If you feel strongly about including a raw vegetable, try something subtle, like endive or sliced fennel with goat cheese.

DIPS, SPREADS, AND JAMS

Jams, jellies, and preserves all transform the sweetness of fruit, making them more palatable for cheese. It's important to choose jam flavors that do not overpower the cheese. Dark fruits such as figs and blackberries are best with more robust cheeses (e.g., aged cheddars and blue cheeses), whereas orange marmalade and strawberry jams are better suited to milder and fresher cheeses. Don't feel tied to fruits, either; carrots and tomatoes make great jams, and you can make spreads out of coffee, spices, chocolates, and so much more. In Spanish cuisine, the classic jam is called *membrillo*, which is made from a pear-like fruit called quince that is too hard and tart to be eaten raw.

The most classic spreadable pairing for cheese is honey. Although honey is very sweet, you often don't notice that it's quite acidic, too, and that sharpness matches the acidic nature of cheese.

Spreads are easy to make, find, and serve, and the options are endless. Savory spreads, such as tapenades and mustards, can amplify the umami flavors in cheese and balance out your board, so it's not overly sweet.

OTHER ACCOMPANIMENTS

Although the options for other accompaniments are infinite, don't put just anything on your cheese board. Accompaniments should either balance out a cheese with a contrast in flavor or texture, or they should complement it by amplifying an existing flavor in a cheese.

Pickles make great accompaniments because they're acidic and fermented, just like cheese, and also because they cut through the fattiness of cheese. Don't feel limited by tradition; although cornichons (also known as gherkins) are a classic accompaniment, pickled green beans, asparagus, apricots, and plums are all wonderful options. You'll find some nontraditional pickle recipes in chapter 7.

Nuts are fatty and salty and go especially well with oily sheep milk cheeses. The classic Spanish cheese nut, the Marcona almond, is sweeter, softer, and rounder than the Californian almond, making it melt in your mouth wonderfully with all cheeses but especially with Spanish cheese. Other great nuts for cheese include walnuts, hazelnuts, and pistachios, which all provide a wonderful crunch to a creamy cheese. Roasting nuts can bring out more of their flavor, and candying them creates the perfect sweet and salty combo.

Other less common but awesome accompaniments include chocolates, caramels, chips, olives, or even tinned fish such as sardines.

BREAD AND CRACKERS

Bread should always be fresh; a good baguette really does not taste the same the next day, which is one reason that crackers are a great choice to serve with cheese. Bread and crackers can function like an accompaniment if you want; for example, a slightly spicy rye might complement a peppery blue.

Ultimately, bread and crackers are primarily a vehicle for the cheese, and simplicity is always a great, safe option. Plain, thin crackers, such as Water Crackers (page 111), with a light dusting of salt are a fantastic choice for any cheese board. With several cheeses, jams, spreads, and other accompaniments, there's no need to introduce a new flavor with your bread or crackers. Because most people choose to take a small piece of bread or a cracker with each bite of cheese, an overpowering or very flavorful bread can detract from your other choices.

EXTRA FLAIR (OPTIONAL)

You can always add a little something extra to jazz up your board. Think about small goodies that add texture and color, or think about what you're serving alongside or after your board and integrate the board into the entire experience.

DRINK PAIRINGS

Each recipe in this book suggests at least one drink pairing. Drink pairings can be difficult with a full cheese board because each cheese is different, but the pairings in this book are curated with the overall flavor profile in mind. When in doubt about wine, choose white because red can overwhelm the cheese, though you will see red wines suggested for several arrangements. Wine might be traditional, but beer, cider, cocktails, and nonalcoholic drinks also make great pairings.

GARNISHES

Garnishes, though not required, can add a little more beauty and flavor to your board. Do *not* put anything inedible on your cheese board: You'd be surprised at what people will try to eat! Herbs add a pop of color and a lovely flavor, especially to young, mild cheeses, such as fresh chèvre or a farmer's cheese. Sprigs of thyme and rosemary look lovely, but chopped parsley, chives, or fresh basil are easier to eat and add both form and function to the board by adding flavor. Edible flowers are a charming addition to any board, especially in the springtime, even if not everyone loves to eat them (make sure to only use food safe flowers or petals). There's not a strong dividing line between accompaniment and garnish; if you use something like candied orange peel, instead of serving it on one side of the board, try placing a few beautifully curled pieces on top of a cheese or jam for a little extra pop.

MAKE IT BEAUTIFUL

A great cheese board not only tastes amazing but looks beautiful, too. Sometimes, it is so beautiful that you don't even want to touch it, but that's when you snap a photo, and then dig in.

CHEESE

Cheese is the centerpiece of your cheese board, so plate your cheese first, and then decide where everything else goes.

Small, whole wheels of cheese are best left whole, and wedges that are easily cut because they're not too hard or crumble into bite-size pieces can be left as they are. Try arranging cut cheese fanned out in a line with each piece slightly overlapping the next. For short, squat triangles, arrange the pieces upright and in two interlaced rows.

COLOR

Including elements of varying colors will really make your cheese board pop.

Although cheese itself doesn't generally span the colors of the rainbow, it's nice to choose some cheeses that aren't all the same color. Chèvre is bright white, an aged cheddar or gouda might be a darker orange, and a Manchego is a paler ivory-yellow. Blue cheese offers a spot of dark bluish green, whereas an ash-covered soft cheese is a stark contrast to just about any other cheese. Some stinky, washed rind cheeses are orange and even a little pink in color.

The accompaniments are where you can really add some color. Fruit can certainly add some spark to a board. Strawberries and raspberries offer a large contrast, but try a blueberry jam for something different.

ARRANGING ELEMENTS

There are two main approaches to arranging a cheese board. The minimalist approach uses more empty space on the board to showcase each element. The lavish approach seeks to cover every inch of the board with ornately presented details. There are arrangements that follow both approaches in this book.

To plate a board in either style, begin by placing some "anchors" on your board. These are larger items, such as a whole wedge or wheel of cheese or ramekins filled with preserves, honey, or nuts. Because these items are larger, it's best to place them on opposite sides of the board, with each near a different corner and one or two near the middle. Disperse them evenly but, for the most pleasing results, keep some asymmetry.

Other elements that are placed in rows, lines, or circles, such as cut cheeses and charcuterie, should be placed next because they take up significant space. Circles of fresh fruit and charcuterie around a ramekin of honey look beautiful. Using different shapes on your board adds attractive variety.

Whole-muscle meats can be presented by lightly folding each slice and placing them in an overlapping row; but if you want to go all out, you can roll each slice in a tight cylinder and place the cylinders upright in a bunch, almost like a bouquet of flowers. Cured sausages are best cut into thin medallions and fanned out in a line or circle. Terrines can be served as a whole loaf or sliced and layered. Bread and crackers can be similarly laid out in a row or circle; they're often not as beautiful as the other elements and can take up a lot of room, so think about using a separate bread basket or cracker tray.

For the minimalist look, leave gaps between each element and don't include too many elements on one board. If you don't own a board large enough to do this, you can make a great arrangement by using three or four smaller boards and feature each cheese on a separate board with the accompaniments that pair best with that cheese. A minimalist look works well on a more intricate or rustic board, such as a handmade wooden board with visible knots. For a more modern minimalist look, try a slate board and label your cheeses with salt chalk.

For a more lavish look, you'll want to fill in all the gaps and go all out in terms of color and texture. Once you've placed your anchors and larger elements on the board, fill in the gaps with accompaniments such as candied nuts, fresh and dried fruits, and chocolates. These elements work best because you can use as much as you need to fill the spaces between the cheeses, meats, and spreads. Try plating an intricate cheese board on a more modern surface, such as marble or petrified wood.

ABOUT THE RECIPES

The recipes in this book are designed to simplify your cheese arrangements. Although you can use the first two chapters of this book to make your own cheese and accompaniments selections, chapters 3, 4, and 5 provide arrangements that have been curated to provide balance, variety, and beauty. The chapters are broken down by board purpose—for appetizers, entertaining, and desserts—but each arrangement includes a further indication of an occasion, season, meal, or flavor profile it might satisfy so that you can scan through and pick the cheese arrangement best suited to your needs.

Each recipe lists the time it takes to prepare the accompaniments, and some recipes indicate that you can or should prepare an accompaniment in advance; these recipes are marked with a "make-ahead" label. Any accompaniment that can be prepared in less than three hours will not be considered a make-ahead item. Additionally, the prep time for water crackers will not be included in the accompaniment prep time when included in the ingredients. Because cheese boards are all about arranging, not cooking, you won't see total cook times for each arrangement. Instead, budget 20 to 30 minutes per board, with more time if you're new to cutting cheese and there are more cheeses, and less time if you're a cheese prep whiz or when there are only one or two cheeses to slice.

Each cheese includes tasting notes in the Glossary (page 113), which can help you in case you wish or need to make a substitution for the cheese itself or for an element you plan to pair with it. Most accompaniments are items you can buy at the grocery store, but every arrangement has at least one element with instructions on how to prepare it yourself—those are in chapters 6 and 7. Happy cooking, arranging, and pairing!

Fresh Burrata Caprese with Arugula, Tomato, and Prosciutto, page 36

CHAPTER 3
APPETIZER BOARDS

BAKED BRIE WITH WINE-POACHED CHERRIES

SERVES 4 / ACCOMPANIMENT PREP TIME: 35 MINUTES / COOK TIME: 25 MINUTES, PLUS 1 MAKE-AHEAD

Baking a whole wheel of brie elevates an already beautiful cheese to something warm, melty, and perfectly decadent. This board is ideal for the fall and winter months when you're craving something cozy or when you want to present something impressive with minimal work.

2 cups Wine-Poached Cherries (page 106)

1 sheet puff pastry, thawed

1 (8-ounce) wheel brie, camembert, or similar brie-style cheese

½ cup walnuts

1 egg, beaten

1 tablespoon water

4 ounces black pepper salami, sliced

20 to 30 crostini

2 tablespoons honey

1. Prepare the poached cherries. Cherries may be prepared up to 2 days in advance.

2. Preheat the oven to 400°F.

3. Unroll the thawed puff pastry. The pastry will enclose the brie, so you might have to roll the shorter side of the pastry out a bit. Place the brie in the center of the pastry. Place the cherries on top of the brie, then add the walnuts.

4. Pull the pastry up and around the brie, so the entire wheel and toppings are covered, and pinch the pastry together to seal. Cut off any extra dough.

5. Make an egg wash by mixing together the egg and water. Brush the pastry with the egg wash to provide shine and seal the pastry.

6. Bake for about 20 minutes, or until the pastry is golden brown.

7. Prepare your board with the salami and crostini on the outside edges, leaving room for the baked brie in the middle.

8. Drizzle the pastry with the honey. Let the brie cool for 5 to 10 minutes before serving.

Drink pairing: This rich and sweet appetizer begs for some dry bubbly. Try a dry sparkling rosé (look for *brut* on the label), which will cut through the richness, making it easier to keep indulging. Pink bubbly has just the right amount of fruity, cherry flavors; plus, it's just plain fun.

Cheesemonger wisdom: When selecting brie in the store, make sure to (gently) poke, prod, and smell the wheel to be sure it has some give. Too firm, and the cheese won't melt well when baked. If you can, unwrap the cheese a little. It should have a mild odor with some sweetness. A very mild ammonia smell is okay (if you have a sensitive nose), but anything overpowering or unpleasant means the cheese is overripe.

FARMHOUSE CHEDDAR AND BUTTER BOARD: APRICOT MUSTARD, THYME, AND DRY-CURED SALAMI

SERVES 2 TO 3 / ACCOMPANIMENT PREP TIME: 50 MINUTES

This simple, rustic board recalls the verdant fields where all cheese and butter originate. Butter brings out the rich, fatty, and creamy flavors of a farmhouse clothbound cheddar that's been rubbed in fat before being wrapped in cloth. This works best with cultured butter, which has been enriched with live cultures, giving it extra flavor. If cultured butter isn't available, look for a pasture-raised or grass-fed unsalted butter.

3 ounces Apricot Mustard (page 84)

5 ounces Farmhouse Cheddar

4 ounces dry-cured salami

4 tablespoons cultured butter

3 ounces honey

2 thyme sprigs

Flaked sea salt

1. Prepare the apricot mustard.

2. Remove the cheddar and butter from the refrigerator about 1 hour before serving to bring to room temperature.

3. If not pre-sliced, slice the salami into thin medallions. Create a layered, curved line of salami diagonally from corner to corner of the board, dividing the board in two.

4. Serve the cheddar in a single piece on one corner of the board. Leave the cloth on the cheddar or peel the cloth back from one corner to show that the cloth is not supposed to be eaten. Use a small cheese fork or paring knife to make a few large crumbles, and place the fork in the block as an indication of how to serve the rest of the block. Put the butter, apricot mustard, and honey in separate ramekins. Place the honey and butter ramekins on the side of the board without the cheddar, and place the apricot mustard ramekin on the other side of the salami near the cheddar.

5. Garnish with a thyme sprig on each side of the board. Sprinkle sea salt flakes on the butter.

Drink pairing: A brown ale pairs perfectly with cheddar, highlighting its caramel notes and balancing the cheddar's sharp acidity with subtle sweetness.

Cheesemonger wisdom: *Cheddaring* is a cheesemaking process that gives cheddar its distinctive sharpness and particular crumble. Ask your cheesemonger for advice if you're not sure whether or not the cheddar you're contemplating buying has been cheddared.

VEGAN CHEESES WITH CANDIED NUTS, APPLE, HONEY, AND DATE CHUTNEY

SERVES 3 TO 4 / ACCOMPANIMENT PREP TIME: 1 HOUR 15 MINUTES

Vegan cheese presents a range of flavors from sweet nuttiness to salty umami savoriness, depending on the base and process of making the cheese. This board showcases some of that range, from tangy, dense Black Ash to mildly smoky and creamy Treeline Classic Aged Nut to more piquant Blue Sheese. This board is great for vegans, those who are lactose intolerant, and dairy lovers alike. Vegan cheese flavors are new to many, so the accompaniments can be more familiar. Nuts highlight the fruity and rich tastes inherent in cheeses made from nuts.

4 ounces Candied Nuts
(page 101)

3 ounces Date Chutney
(page 90)

Miyoko's Black Ash

Treeline Classic Aged
Nut Cheese

Bute Island Blue French
Style Sheese Wedge

2 ounces honey

1 apple, thinly sliced
(a sweeter variety such
as Pink Lady)

1. Prepare the candied nuts. While the nuts are in the oven, prepare the date chutney.

2. Place each of the three cheeses on a different part of the board. Cut a small wedge in each of the two wheel-shaped cheeses (Miyoko's Black Ash and Treeline Classic), leaving the small wedges where they were cut as an indication of how to cut the cheese.

3. Put the honey and date chutney into separate small ramekins. Place the honey close to the Black Ash and the date chutney near the Blue Sheese.

4. Layer the apple slices, creating a line of apple around one ramekin and reaching the other. You may not need to use the entire apple.

5. Fill the empty spots on the board with the candied nuts.

Drink pairing: Nutty, herbal white wines pair well with nut cheeses. White wines from the Alps are often full-bodied and herbaceous with a nice touch of minerality. Grape varietals from this region to try include kerner, Aligoté, and chardonnay.

Substitution tip: Vegan cheeses can be hard to find, but they're becoming more popular. If you are unable to find the three recommended in this arrangement, look for substitutions that are varied in style to create a balanced board. The key to a good vegan board is finding a variety of high-quality vegan cheeses—look for an artisan label.

SPANISH TAPAS WITH MONTE ENEBRO, MANCHEGO, AND SMOKED IDIAZABAL

SERVES 4 / ACCOMPANIMENT PREP TIME: 1 HOUR 15 MINUTES

In Spain, tapas are small bites meant to be eaten after work before a traditionally late dinner between 9 p.m. and 11 p.m. This board is inspired by common Spanish tapas ingredients, transformed into an easy pre-dinner snack. Membrillo is also known as quince paste; purchase it in a block, if possible. Use Manzanilla olives; they're green, tangy, and nutty.

6 Balsamic Artichokes (page 107), halved

5 ounces Monte Enebro

5 ounces Aged Manchego

5 ounces Smoked Idiazabal

4 ounces jamón serrano

3 ounces membrillo

¼ cup mixed olives

4 ounces Marcona almonds

Olive oil crackers

1. Prepare the balsamic artichokes. While the artichokes marinate, begin to prepare the cheeses and the board.

2. Using a cheese wire, slice the Monte Enebro into medallions. Cut the Aged Manchego and Smoked Idiazabal into small triangles. Loosely fold each slice of jamón serrano in half. Slice the membrillo into small, thin squares, about 1 inch on each edge and less than ¼ inch thick.

3. Place the olives in a ramekin off-center on the board. Fan out each cut cheese in a curved line on a different part of the board. Layer the sliced membrillo and folded jamón similarly.

4. Place two artichoke halves in each of the empty spaces on the board. Evenly distribute a few almonds here and there throughout the board. Add the crackers.

5. Serve with toothpicks.

Drink pairing: Continue your Spanish sojourn with a bottle of juicy Tempranillo with notes of vanilla, tobacco, dried fig, and cherry. These cheeses can stand up to the bold, savory flavors of Tempranillo. Try a crianza style for a fruit-forward delight, or take it to the next level with a Reserva for a bit more oak and oomph.

Cheesemonger wisdom: Blue mold can only grow where there's oxygen, and Monte Enebro takes advantage of that. It has a thick, creamy interior without air pockets, so the blue mold that's added only grows on the outside, making the cheese subtly spicy and mostly tangy, bright, and citric, like other young chèvres.

FRESH BURRATA CAPRESE WITH ARUGULA, TOMATO, AND PROSCIUTTO

SERVES 4 / ACCOMPANIMENT PREP TIME: 0 MINUTES

Burrata is magically rich and wonderful. This melt-in-your-mouth cheese is made like mozzarella by stretching fresh curd, and then wrapping that supple cheese into a ball and stuffing it with more cheese that has been soaked in cream. The result? A delicate pouch that explodes with fatty goodness when you cut into it. Dress it up a little, and you'll have a stunning and delicious—if slightly messy—board.

1 cup arugula

¼ cup olive oil, divided

1 heirloom tomato, thinly sliced

8 slices (3 to 4 ounces) prosciutto

1 (8-ounce) ball burrata

Flaked sea salt

2 tablespoons balsamic vinegar

5 fresh basil leaves

4 (1-inch-thick) slices ciabatta

1. Lightly toss the arugula in 1 tablespoon of the olive oil.

2. Evenly cover a round platter or board with the arugula.

3. Place the tomato slices in a tight, overlapping circle in the center of the board.

4. Fold the prosciutto slices in half and arrange them in a larger circle around the tomatoes, spacing them out evenly.

5. Place the burrata in the center of the tomato circle. Sprinkle it with a pinch of salt. Using a spoon, drizzle the balsamic vinegar over the burrata, then drizzle with 2 tablespoons of the olive oil.

6. Garnish the board with the basil leaves.

7. Heat a grill pan over medium-high heat. Brush both sides of each slice of ciabatta with the remaining 1 tablespoon of olive oil, and sprinkle them with a small pinch of sea salt on each slice. Grill the bread on each side for 2 to 3 minutes, until slightly charred. Place the grilled bread on the board and serve immediately with a sharp knife and toothpicks.

Drink pairing: An Italian prosecco is just about the best way to jazz up this mouthwatering appetizer. The bubbles work well with the decadent cream of the burrata, and the wine's fruity aromas contrast with the peppery arugula and salty meat and cheese.

Cheesemonger wisdom: Burrata, like mozzarella, is a style of cheese called *pasta filata*, which means "spun paste" in Italian. Pasta filata cheeses are known as "stretched curd" because cheesemakers literally stretch warm, softened curds into long strings, giving it a characteristic melty stretchiness—the perfect pizza cheese!

GOAT THREE WAYS: SOFT SAINTE MAURE, GOUDA, BLUE, AND DUCK PROSCIUTTO

SERVES 3 TO 4 / ACCOMPANIMENT PREP TIME: 1 HOUR 30 MINUTES, PLUS 3 MAKE-AHEADS

To some, "goat cheese" has become synonymous with fresh chèvre. This board will prove otherwise! Goat cheese has certain characteristics; it's bright, citric, grassy, and peppery. But it can be made into a fresh, soft, hard, or blue cheese.

¼ cup Beet Jam with Rosemary, Thyme, and Honey (page 76)

½ cup candied walnuts (see Candied Nuts on page 101)

¼ cup Lemon Curd (page 86)

4 ounces (½ log) Sainte Maure

1 (4-ounce) wedge Capra Verde

5 ounces Goat Gouda

¼ cup thinly sliced duck prosciutto

1 baguette, sliced

1. Prepare the beet jam and candied walnuts. While they're cooking, prepare the lemon curd. Alternatively, the beet jam may be canned months in advance, and the candied walnuts may be prepared up to 2 weeks in advance.

2. Using a cheese wire or unflavored floss, slice the Sainte Maure into thin medallions. Make an arch of the slices by slightly overlapping the medallions on one corner of the board. Fill a ramekin with the beet jam and place it in the curve of the arch.

3. Put the lemon curd in another ramekin on the opposite side of the board. Nearby, but not touching, place the Capra Verde wedge with a small cheese knife in it for serving.

4. Cut the Goat Gouda into long, thin triangles and line them up near the center of the board, between the Sainte Maure and Capra Verde. Place them on their long edges in a zipper pattern so that the tips are in the center of the pattern and the short edge of the triangles are on the outside.

5. Fan out the duck prosciutto slices in a line. Put the candied walnuts in three separate small piles on different parts of the board. If there's room, add the sliced baguette to the board, or serve it on the side.

Drink pairing: High-acid white wines, such as sauvignon blanc, are classic goat cheese pairings. For a truly traditional drink pairing, try Sancerre, a sauvignon blanc from the Loire Valley in France. The matching levels of acidity make for an invigorating pairing full of zip.

Substitution tip: If Sainte Maure isn't available, any ash-covered soft goat cheese will do. Others to try include Valençay, Selles-sur-Cher, Vermont Creamery Bonne Bouche, Andante Acapella, and Capriole Sofia. Cypress Grove's famous Humboldt Fog is bit more aged with a bloomier rind and will work wonderfully.

BOLD AND STRONG: STINKY ÉPOISSES, AROMATIC APPENZELLER, AND SPICY CABRALES BLUE

SERVES 4 / ACCOMPANIMENT PREP TIME: 1 MAKE-AHEAD

This board is for the adventurous! Époisses is so stinky and meaty that legend says it's illegal to carry it on the Paris Metro. Appenzeller is herbaceous with a slight spice derived from an herbed brine cure. Cabrales is one of the most powerful blues. Each cheese on this board is intense and complex, so the selected accompaniments are simple but strong enough to hold up to these robust flavors.

3 tablespoons Pickled Fennel (page 97)

2 tablespoons honey

1 (8.8-ounce) wheel Époisses

5 ounces Appenzeller

4 slices (½-inch thick) pâté de campagne

4 ounces Cabrales

½ cup almonds

1 baguette, cut into ¼-inch-thick slices

1. Prepare the pickled fennel in advance.

2. Put the honey in a ramekin near the center of the board and place the pickled fennel in a ramekin off to one side.

3. Remove the lid from the Époisses box and serve the cheese with a small teaspoon placed in the box. Situate the cheese on the side of board opposite the fennel.

4. Cut the Appenzeller into thin sticks and layer them to form a rectangle near the fennel ramekin.

5. On the opposite side of the fennel ramekin, layer the pâté slices.

6. Place the Cabrales wedge equidistant from the other two cheeses, so the three cheeses form a triangle on the board.

7. Fill the empty spots on the board with the almonds and baguette slices.

Drink pairing: When in doubt, an off-dry riesling is a great cheese board choice because its sweetness balances out the salt in the cheeses. Although it may be the answer to nearly any board, it pairs particularly well with a stinky and salty cheese, such as Époisses, because of its sweetness and honey-like qualities, as well as with Appenzeller because of its floral notes.

Substitution tip: If you can't find these exact cheeses, know that you're looking for a soft, gooey, stinky cheese in place of the Époisses, such as Maroilles, Livarot, or Red Hawk. In place of Appenzeller, an aged Comté or another Alpine can do. If you can't find Cabrales but see Valdéon, know that the latter is modeled on the former. If you see neither, Roquefort will carry a good punch, too.

BEER LOVER'S BOARD: LEAF-WRAPPED CHEESE, GUINNESS CHEDDAR, YOUNG GOUDA, AND BEER MUSTARD

MAKE-AHEAD / SERVES 2 TO 4 / ACCOMPANIMENT PREP TIME: 1 MAKE-AHEAD

A cheese board for beer lovers! Wine and cheese might be more traditional, but beer complements cheese well—sometimes even better than wine. The natural carbonation of beer cuts through the fat in cheese and provides texture. The malt backbone of many beers provides a balanced sweetness to pair with salty cheese, and the hoppy aromas highlight grassy and floral notes in cheese. Beer is very varied, and unlike wine, which is only made from grapes, beer can benefit from the creativity of many added ingredients. Pairing beer and cheese is fun, exciting, and limitless.

2 tablespoons Whole-Grain Beer Mustard (page 91)

1 (4-ounce) ball Up in Smoke, River's Edge, or similar leaf-wrapped cheese

4 ounces Guinness Cheddar

4 ounces Young Gouda

4 ounces Genoa salami, thinly sliced

3 small grape bunches (about 30 grapes)

3 ounces salted pistachios, shelled

20 to 30 plain or salted Water Crackers (page 111) or store-bought

1. Prepare the beer mustard at least 3 days in advance. Serve it in a ramekin on one corner of the board.

2. In the opposite corner, place the leaf-wrapped cheese, unwrapping the leaves so the cheese is exposed but still sitting on the leaves.

3. Cut the cheddar into long, thin triangles, and cut the gouda into small, squat triangles.

4. Layer the cheddar triangles in a line in the middle of the board, and interlock the gouda triangles so they are upright, forming an arch on the corner of the board around the mustard-filled ramekin.

5. Layer the salami slices in an arch that follows the form of the leaf-wrapped cheese.

6. Place the grape bunches in the gaps on the board, then fill any remaining empty spaces with small piles of pistachios.

7. Serve with the crackers on the side or on the board, as space allows.

continued ›

Beer Lover's Board *continued*

Drink pairing: Rich and robust beers are not always well suited to cheese because they can be overpowering, but the three cheeses on this board can stand up to a heavier beer style. Try a porter; it's lighter than a heavy stout but has some richness with notes of chocolate, coffee, and caramel balanced with bready malt and light hoppy bitterness. An often overlooked style of beer, extra special bitter (ESB) is a wonderfully balanced beer. It's lighter than porter but has a bit more body than an amber ale. Despite the name, it's not especially bitter, and it has a stronger malt backbone that's delightfully balanced by a nice mild bitter finish. These beers won't overpower any cheese and will bring out the sweet, fruity flavors on the board.

Cheesemonger wisdom: Wrapping cheeses in leaves is an old tradition that results in a beautiful appearance. Originally used as a method to protect cheeses against insects, leaf wrapping imparts earthy and autumnal flavors. Up in Smoke uses smoked maple leaves for a smoky flavor profile, whereas other cheeses are wrapped in leaves soaked in alcohols like bourbon. Other leaf-wrapped cheeses include Banon from France, Capriole Creamery's O'Banon from Indiana, and Hoja Santa from Texas.

FOR A DINNER ROAST: CASATICA, RACLETTE, MIDDLEBURY BLUE, AND HAZELNUT AGRODOLCE

SERVES 2 TO 4 / ACCOMPANIMENT PREP TIME: 50 MINUTES, PLUS 1 MAKE-AHEAD

Three very different cheeses star on this board. They aren't too wild, but they have enough substance to stand up to a medium-bodied red wine and to eat alongside roasted red meats and veggies. Casatica, a soft bloomy rind traditionally made in Italy from water buffalo milk, is robust and fatty. Raclette, known for its melting properties, is wonderful all on its own; it's nutty and pungent with a supple texture. Middlebury Blue is milky and mellow, veined with a pleasantly spicy blue, and it crumbles just the right amount.

2 ounces Fall Spice Infused Honey (page 82)

15 to 20 Baked Butternut Squash Chips (page 110)

¼ cup Hazelnut Agrodolce (page 80)

5 ounces Raclette

4 ounces Casatica

4 ounces Middlebury Blue

1 baguette, sliced

1. Prepare the accompaniments. All may be made in advance, but the honey must be made at least 5 days ahead. Begin by preparing the squash chips, and while they are roasting, start the agrodolce.

2. Cut the raclette into long, thin rectangles. Cut the Casatica loaf into slices, then cut each slice like a pizza to make triangular wedges.

3. Put the honey and agrodolce in two ramekins and place them on opposite sides of the board. Arrange the Casatica triangles in a layered arch around the ramekin of honey. Arrange the raclette rectangles in two interlocking lines near the ramekin of agrodolce. Place the wedge of Middlebury Blue on the third side of the board.

4. In the middle of the board, layer the squash chips in a circle. Serve the baguette on the side.

Drink pairing: A fruit-forward red wine, such as a pinot noir, with balanced earthiness and cranberry-like acidity will complement the cheeses on this board, and any extra glasses will pair well with a roasted meat and vegetable main course. Try a wine from the Willamette Valley in Oregon, which will be a bit more rustic than a California pinot noir.

Cheesemonger wisdom: Water buffalo are more similar to the dairy cow than they are to the American bison. Native to India, China, and Southeast Asia, these popular animals are now found on every continent. In Italy, in particular, buffalo are prized for their milk, which is higher in fat and protein than cow's milk, giving cheeses, like Casatica, their luscious texture.

FARM AND FIELD: CAMEMBERT, LIMBURGER, AND TOMME DE SAVOIE WITH MOUSSE PÂTÉ AND TRUFFLED MUSHROOM SPREAD

SERVES 3 TO 4 / ACCOMPANIMENT PREP TIME: 30 MINUTES

Take a trip to the country farm with the rustic, barnyard flavors of this board. Camembert is a little more mushroomy, garlicky, and earthy than its brie cousin, but it has all the same creamy lusciousness. Limburger, a classic washed rind cheese, was originally made by Trappist monks in what is now Belgium, the Netherlands, and Germany and is all about pungency. Round the selection out with a tomme, a milky grassy wheel that smells like it's just been hanging out in a cave because, well, it has been.

¼ cup Truffled Mushroom Spread (page 79)

5 ounces Limburger

5 ounces Tomme de Savoie

½ wheel (4 to 5 ounces) Camembert

4 ounces mousse pâté

3 ounces (about 15) dilly beans (pickled green beans)

3 ounces salted potato chips (about 3 individual-size snack bags)

1. Prepare the mushroom spread.

2. Cut the Limburger into long, thin triangles and cut the tomme into thin rectangles.

3. Place the Camembert on one corner of the board. Cut one small piece out of it and leave it in place, indicating how to cut the Camembert while maintaining its semicircle shape.

4. Place the mushroom spread in a ramekin near the Camembert. Place the mousse pâté in a ramekin on the other side of the board.

5. Layer the tomme rectangles in a line, curving around the ramekin of pâté. Arrange the Limburger triangles in a curved line in the center of the board.

6. Create two stacks of dilly beans on either side of the Limburger.

7. In two other corners of the board, pile on the chips.

Drink pairing: Try a beverage that's equally expressive of this board's fermented flavors. A Gueuze is a blended beer made from mixing three sour batches of beer—aged one, two, and three years, respectively—for a complex and layered tartness. Pétillant naturel, or Pét-Nat, is a great wine option with its yeasty flavor and light fizz.

Cheesemonger wisdom: Legend says that stinky cheeses, such as the Limburger, originated because of the monks' dedication to cleanliness; a monk saw mold growing on cheese and began washing it, which resulted in an orangish rind and meaty flavor. Other Trappist washed-rind cheeses that you can use in place of Limburger include Chimay Red, Port Salut, and Père Joseph.

Fan Favorites, page 56

CHAPTER 4

PARTY PLATTERS

FALL FLAVORS: HONEY-CHÈVRE, BARK-WRAPPED BRIE, AGED MANCHEGO, AND CREAMY GORGONZOLA

MAKE-AHEAD / SERVES 8 / ACCOMPANIMENT PREP TIME: 2 HOURS 25 MINUTES, PLUS 1 MAKE-AHEAD

Just like fruits, cheese is seasonal, too. This board is all about using ingredients that are best in the fall. Although this board has a lot of accompaniments to prepare, you can save time by picking a few up from the store. This is a great arrangement if you don't want to cut a lot of cheese: Three of the four cheeses on this board don't require any prep.

4 ounces Fall Spice Infused Honey (page 82)

4 ounces Apple Butter (page 88)

2½ cups Baked Butternut Squash Chips (page 110)

1 (9-ounce) wheel Jasper Hill Harbison, or any brie-style cheese wrapped in bark

1 (8-ounce) log Honey-Flavored Chèvre

½ pound Gorgonzola Cremificato

3 Bosc pears, each cut into 8 even slices

1 tablespoon freshly squeezed lemon juice (optional)

1 (¾-pound) wedge Aged Manchego

½ pound pâté de campagne, sliced

½ baguette, cut into ¼-inch slices

1. Prepare the accompaniments. All may be made in advance, but the honey must be made at least 5 days ahead. Start the apple butter and let it simmer while you prepare the butternut squash chips.

2. When the accompaniments are done, start your arrangement by evenly distributing the anchors across the board: the Harbison, chèvre, gorgonzola, apple butter (in a ramekin), and spiced honey (in a ramekin).

3. Arrange the pear slices in a winding line so that each slice slightly overlaps the previous one. Start the line around one ramekin and curve it so that it reaches a nearby anchor. Drizzle the lemon juice (if using) over the pear slices to prevent them from browning.

4. Cut the rind off the top and bottom of the manchego. Leaving the rind on the side of the wedge, cut it into ¼-inch-thick triangles, following the shape of the cheese.

5. Arrange the pâté slices, like the pears, in a slightly overlapping line. Then, arrange the manchego triangles and baguette slices similarly.

6. Fill any gaps on the cheese board with the squash chips.

Drink pairing: Red wines from the Southwest region of France are earthy, making them perfect for fall, just like this cheese board! Cabernet franc is a sure bet, and a French malbec (known as côt) will also complement this board nicely. Or choose an apple cider like Isastegi cider from the Basque region or Shacksbury cider, made in Vermont in the traditional Basque style.

Substitution tip: You can easily swap in a vegan cashew "chèvre" instead of the Honey Chèvre. You can also find this vegan alternative flavored with herbs or plain, in which case you can drizzle honey on top.

SPRINGTIME BLOOM: TÊTE DE MOINE, HUDSON FLOWER, ALP BLOSSOM, AND CASHEL BLUE

SERVES 8 / ACCOMPANIMENT PREP TIME: 2 HOURS 15 MINUTES

Spring means flowers, and this cheese board is full of them. Tête de Moine looks like a flower, Hudson Flower and Alp Blossom are covered in real flowers, and Cashel Blue is a butter bomb with a floral aroma. Top the board off with some seasonal fruit jam and culinary grade flowers for a blooming cheese board bursting with color, brightness, and harmony.

¼ cup Candied Lemon Peel (page 102)

½ wheel (about 15 ounces) Tête de Moine

8 ounces rosemary-cured lonza

¼ cup strawberry-rhubarb jam

1 (12-ounce) wheel Hudson Flower

10 ounces Alp Blossom

8 ounces Cashel Blue

¼ cup almonds

1 ounce assorted edible flowers

2 baguettes, cut into ¼-inch-thick slices

25 Water Crackers (page 111) or store-bought

1. Prepare the candied lemon peel. While lemon peel is simmering, prepare the board.

2. Using a cheese curler (*girolle*), shave the Tête de Moine into rosettes. If you do not have a cheese curler, the store may sell you pre-shaved rosettes upon request. If this is not possible either, you can use a flat knife like a cleaver to carefully scrape the top of the cheese in a thin layer that will curl up into a flower-like rosette.

3. Arrange the rosettes on one corner of the board. Roll each slice of rosemary lonza into a cone and lay them in a pile on the other side of the board.

4. Spoon the jam into a ramekin and place it near the Tête de Moine.

5. Place the Hudson Flower near the middle of the board, cutting and partially removing one slice from the wheel. Cut the Alp Blossom into long, thin rectangles and arrange them in a line in an empty spot on the board, as far away from the other anchor items as possible. Place the wedge of Cashel Blue in any remaining large space.

6. Fill the gaps between the meat and cheeses with the almonds and candied lemon peel.

7. Garnish the board with the edible flowers.

8. Serve the baguette and crackers in a basket, or if there is some room on the edge of the board, you can layer the crackers along one side.

continued ›

Springtime Bloom *continued*

Drink pairing: Use any leftover flowers to garnish a floral cocktail. Aviation is a gin-based cocktail made with crème de violette, which gives it a pretty lavender hue and a wonderful herbaceousness with bright acidity from the lemon juice.

Gewürztraminer is riesling's more extravagant cousin. It is incredibly aromatic, almost like perfume, smelling of lychee and wildflowers. Its natural sweetness makes it a great match for cheese and the perfect wine to pair with a flowery board.

Cheesemonger wisdom: Floral cheeses can be hard to find, but their striking beauty and interesting flavors make a big impression. Other flower- or herb-covered cheeses include Cabra Romero, Fleur de Maquis, and Flower Marie. If you can't find any flower cheeses, you can use a bloomy rind, brie-style, or chèvre and directly press the edible flowers into their rinds.

WINTER WARMTH: SHEEP BRIE, GRAN QUESO, IRISH CHEDDAR, OSSAU-IRATY, AND SAINT AGUR BLUE

SERVES 8 TO 10 / ACCOMPANIMENT PREP TIME: 2 HOURS 10 MINUTES, PLUS 2 MAKE-AHEADS

Cold weather calls for thick blankets and layers. Winter cheese styles are high in fat, and full of warming, aromatic spices. Sheep cheese is naturally robust, brie-style cheeses are lavish, and a blue, such as Saint Agur, is rich with a mild kick. Gran Queso is rubbed in paprika and cinnamon, and Irish Cheddar toes the line between sweet and savory, making this cheese board comforting on a cooler night.

15 to 18 slices
Dried Blood Oranges
(page 109)

1 cup candied walnuts
(see Candied Nuts on
page 101)

1 pound Sheep Brie

10 ounces Ossau-Iraty

12 ounces Gran Queso

10 ounces Irish Cheddar

8 ounces Saint Agur Blue

8 ounces lamb
prosciutto

6 ounces duck rillettes

20 fruit and nut crisps

1 cup dried Mission figs

¼ cup pomegranate
seeds

30 Water Crackers
(page 111) or
store-bought

1. Prepare the blood orange slices and candied walnuts. Both can be made ahead.

2. Cut the cheeses into different shapes. The brie can be sliced into small wedges, the Ossau-Iraty can be served in small rectangles, and the Gran Queso can be cut into triangles. The cheddar can be served with a cheese fork for crumbling, and the blue can be served with a small brie knife.

3. Place each cheese on a different part of the board, in a quincunx arrangement (like the dots on the 5 face of a die), but each slightly off-center.

4. Layer the prosciutto slices in one corner of the board, and place the duck rillettes (in a ramekin) on the opposite side.

5. In two different places on the board, layer the blood orange slices; do the same with the fruit and nut crisps.

6. Fill in the gaps on the board with the candied walnuts and figs. Garnish the blue and brie with the pomegranate seeds for a pop of color and brightness.

7. Serve the crackers in a basket on the side, or, if there's room, layered along one edge of the board.

continued ›

Drink pairing: The density of the sheep cheeses, the cinnamon on the Gran Queso, and the spice and fat in the Saint Agur all call for a red wine with a bit of body. This board can stand up to something with tannic structure and a bit of alcohol. Nebbiolo, a grape native to Northern Italy's Piedmont region, has grippy tannins, good acidity, and cherry-like fruits with a leathery backbone. When searching for Nebbiolo-based wines, look for Barolo and Barbaresco on the label.

Cheesemonger wisdom: Sheep's milk is higher in fat than cow's milk, making it super buttery. When the milk is left out at room temperature for serving, the butterfat will often rise to the surface, leaving an oily sheen. The high fat content means sheep's cheese is often dense and thick textured with flavors of oil, butter, and nuts reminiscent of pine nuts, Marcona almonds, and walnuts.

SUMMER FRESHNESS: RICOTTA, CHÈVRE LOG, GRAFTON CHEDDAR, MEULE DE SAVOIE, AND GORGONZOLA DOLCE

SERVES 8 / ACCOMPANIMENT PREP TIME: 1 TO 2 HOURS

One of the best parts of summer is the excuse to indulge in fresh berries, invigorating drinks, and bright and creamy cheeses. This selection includes the fresh styles of ricotta and chèvre; a distinctively bright cheddar that's reminiscent of freshly cut grass; an Alpine that's full of floral, herbaceous flavors; and a sweet blue that's as velvety as ice cream.

4 ounces Tomato Conserve (page 87)

10 ounces Grafton Cheddar

10 ounces Meule de Savoie

8 ounces Fresh Ricotta

1 (8-ounce) fresh Chèvre log

8 ounces Gorgonzola Dolce

1 tablespoon honey

1 cup diced watermelon

¼ cup pickled red onion

1 cup fresh berries, such as blueberries, halved strawberries, and/or raspberries

½ cup almonds

10 fresh mint leaves

2 baguettes, cut into ¼-inch pieces

1. Prepare the Tomato Conserve.

2. Cut the cheddar into thin rectangles and the Meule de Savoie into long, thin triangles.

3. Place the ricotta (in a small bowl) in the top left corner of the board. Working diagonally toward the bottom right corner (but not exactly in a straight line), place the cheeses in the following order: ricotta, chèvre, cheddar rectangles (in a layered circle), Meule triangles (in a layered line), and then the gorgonzola.

4. Put the honey, watermelon, and pickled red onion in three separate ramekins. Place the watermelon near the ricotta, the honey near the gorgonzola, and the red onion off to the side, close to the cheddar and Meule.

5. Fill the gaps on the board with the berries and almonds.

6. Use some mint leaves to garnish the ricotta and watermelon, and place the rest directly on the board for color.

7. Serve the crusty baguettes in a cloth-lined basket.

Drink pairing: A quintessential summer beer, Berliner Weisse is low in alcohol, so you can keep sipping it through the heat. It has crisp acidity and is refreshingly tart; it's a great starter sour beer for the sour-curious! The beer has fruity aromas with a wheat backbone, so it'll complement every bite from this board.

Cheesemonger wisdom: Gorgonzola is known as a pungent but decadent blue that's often crumbled in salads or used to make blue cheese dip. Really though, there's a big range of gorgonzolas that can be divided into two main types: Gorgonzola Dolce and Gorgonzola Piccante. The Dolce kind is sweet, fudgy, and richly textured, with less intense blue. The Piccante is a bit spicier, piquant, and often a little more on the crumbly side.

DECADENCE AND BUBBLES: DOUBLE- AND TRIPLE-CRÈME BRIE, AGED COMTÉ, AND QUADRELLO DI BUFALA

SERVES 8 / ACCOMPANIMENT PREP TIME: 0 MINUTES

Big celebrations call for decadence, a little splurging, and, of course, sparkling wine. These cheeses are luscious, rich, and paired with wowing accompaniments that will make this cheese board as exciting and memorable as whatever you're celebrating—even if you're just excited that it's Tuesday!

10 ounces Aged (12+ months) Comté

10 ounces Quadrello di Bufala

1 (8-ounce) wheel double-crème brie

12 ounces Brillat-Savarin, or other triple-crème brie

¼ cup Tarragon-Champagne Pickled Strawberries (page 96)

8 ounces pork rillettes

¼ cup hazelnuts

½ cup candied fruit

50 Water Crackers (page 111) or store-bought

1. Cut the Comté into long, thin sticks. Cut the quadrello into thin rectangles. Using a brie knife, cut one wedge out of the wheel of double-crème brie, and replace it; arrange the prepared wheel near one of the edges of the board.

2. Place the Brillat-Savarin near the center of the board with the strawberries (in a ramekin) nearby.

3. Near the edges of the board, arrange the Comté pieces in a curved line and the quadrello in an arch or circle.

4. Place the rillettes in a small ramekin or dish far from the cheeses.

5. Surround the Comté with the hazelnuts placed directly on the board.

6. Put the candied fruit around the quadrello.

7. Fill the rest of the board with the water crackers, layered.

Drink pairing: Break out the bubbly for this one. If you can swing it, go for real deal Champagne. It has finer bubbles than other styles of sparkling wine, which makes it delicate and refined. Those small bubbles pair nicely with the lusciousness of the two brie styles and with a cheese as lavish as Quadrello di Bufala. Plus, you'll feel extra fancy.

Cheesemonger wisdom: Jean Anthelme Brillat-Savarin was a famous French gastronomist and food writer from the early nineteenth century who loved bloomy rind brie but yearned for a cheese that was even richer, fattier, and more like butter. And so, the most decadent cheese was named after him: a triple-crème brie that's the perfect marriage of silk, cream, and tang.

ITALIAN ANTIPASTO WITH LA TUR, TALEGGIO, ASIAGO D'ALLEVO, PECORINO TOSCANO, AND AGED PROVOLONE

SERVES 8 TO 10 / ACCOMPANIMENT PREP TIME: 1 HOUR 15 MINUTES

An antipasto board is the traditional start to a big Italian meal and is filled with small bites of great flavor. This platter is a riff on the classic antipasto plate. It's cheese-centric and celebrates styles from the many regions of Italy, from multiple provinces in the north, where you'll find La Tur, Taleggio, and Asiago; to Tuscany in Central Italy, and farther south near Naples, where the best provolone hails from.

1 cup Balsamic Artichokes (page 107)

¾ cup Roasted Red Peppers (page 103)

¼ cup Green Olive Pesto (page 92)

8 ounces Asiago d'Allevo

8 ounces Pecorino Toscano

8 ounces Aged Provolone

¼ cup mixed olives

1 (8-ounce) wheel La Tur

8 ounces prosciutto

8 ounces coppa

8 ounces Taleggio

10 fresh basil leaves

1 loaf ciabatta, cut into ¼-inch slices, halved

20 olive oil crostini

1. Prepare the balsamic artichokes, and while they marinate, prepare the roasted red peppers and olive pesto.

2. Cut the asiago into long, thin triangles; the pecorino into small, thin rectangles; and the provolone into small, squat triangles.

3. Put the pesto and olives in separate ramekins, and arrange them on different sides of the board. Find a corner to place the La Tur.

4. Arrange the meats on opposite ends of the board from each other: fold the prosciutto slices and layer them in a line, and scrunch the coppa pieces to arrange in a circular pile.

5. Going in a circle from the La Tur, arranging the cut cheeses in layered lines or arches, place the cheeses in the following order: Taleggio, asiago, pecorino, provolone.

6. Use the artichokes, red peppers, and olives to fill the gaps directly on the board, making sure each component is in 2 or 3 places across the board.

7. Garnish the board with the basil leaves, and serve the bread and crostini on the side.

continued ›

Italian Antipasto *continued*

Drink pairing: Sangiovese is a beautiful grape that makes wines with a range of flavors: some rustic and savory, others more fruit-forward. In general, Sangiovese has cherry notes and is known for its good acidity, which makes it suitable for a variety of cheeses. Try a Chianti Classico, which is a blend of at least 80 percent Sangiovese grapes with other local grapes.

Cheesemonger wisdom: Parmigiano-Reggiano is a cheese that must be made according to very strict rules and only in certain parts of the Emilia-Romagna and Lombardy provinces. Other Italian cheeses, such as asiago, have similar rules. Pecorino refers to any firm Italian cheese made from sheep's milk and is particularly great on pasta. Some pecorinos, such as Pecorino Toscano, have further specificities as to how they're made.

EARTH AND SMOKE: CAMEMBERT, TALEGGIO, MIMOLETTE, SMOKED GOUDA, AND MOUNTAIN GORGONZOLA

SERVES 8 / ACCOMPANIMENT PREP TIME: 1 HOUR 5 MINUTES

Each cheese on this board brings something strong to the table, from earth to funk to caramel to smoke to spice. Tying it all up are some spicy meats, sweet and sour foods, and playful textures. Your taste buds will be buzzing with wonder.

3 ounces Hot Pepper Honey (page 83)

4 ounces Sweet and Tangy Sautéed Shallots (page 98)

8 strips Candied Bacon (page 99), quartered

½ pound Mimolette

½ pound Smoked Gouda

½ pound Mountain Gorgonzola

1 (8-ounce) wheel Camembert

½ pound Taleggio

½ pound chorizo, thinly sliced

½ cup dried apples

½ cup almonds

1. Prepare the honey, and while the honey simmers, prepare the shallots and candied bacon.

2. Cut the Mimolette into small rectangles and the gouda into thin triangles. Crumble the gorgonzola. The Camembert and Taleggio can be served whole with one sample wedge cut out of each cheese.

3. Put the honey and shallots into separate ramekins. Place the honey ramekin in the center of the board and the shallot ramekin off to the side.

4. Stack the Mimolette rectangles into a large, layered larger rectangle radiating out from the honey ramekin. Place the Taleggio and Camembert by the shallots on opposite sides of the ramekin.

5. Layer the gouda triangles in an unused corner of the board, and stack the bacon nearby. Pile the gorgonzola crumbles in another corner. Layer the chorizo slices in an arch facing inward toward the center of the board.

6. Fill in the gaps on the board with the apples and almonds.

Drink pairing: Shiraz is the same grape as syrah, but shiraz is used to describe wines specifically from Australia and South Africa. Syrah/shiraz is dark in color and, much like this cheese board, rich in flavor. A shiraz will be more intense in spice, oak, and alcohol, and still rich in bright fruit flavors like black cherries and black currants.

Cheesemonger wisdom: Mimolette is an iconic cheese that's bright orange and spherical. Perhaps less visible, but more famously known—it's also been munched by mites. Yes, microscopic bugs feed on this wheel, giving the aged versions a moonlike surface with holes. But not to worry, the mites are mostly brushed off before the cheese is ready for sale, and whatever mites remain are neither visible nor harmful, nor can you taste them.

FAN FAVORITES: ROBIOLA, YOUNG GOUDA, YOUNG MANCHEGO, AND IRISH CHEDDAR

SERVES 6 TO 8 / ACCOMPANIMENT PREP TIME: 1 HOUR 15 MINUTES

These cheeses will impress, but they are still familiar enough to please most people. The younger cheeses are more approachable than their aged counterparts, and Irish cheddar is more recognizable to the American palate as cheddar than a British-style clothbound cheddar. Robiola has a brie-style texture but is mellower in flavor and has a thinner rind.

¼ cup Candied Nuts (page 101)

¼ cup Date Chutney (page 90)

8 ounces Young Gouda (aged 2 to 4 months)

8 ounces Young Manchego (aged 3 to 4 months)

8 ounces Irish Cheddar

8 ounces sweet soppressata, sliced

3 tablespoons honey

1 (8-ounce) wheel Robiola

20 Water Crackers (page 111) or store-bought

6 to 8 bunches (about 15) green grapes

8 ounces prosciutto, sliced

1 baguette, cut into ¼-inch slices

1. Prepare the candied nuts, and while they are in the oven, prepare the date chutney.

2. Cut the gouda into long, thin triangles; the manchego into squat, thin triangles; and the cheddar into long, thin rectangles.

3. Layer the soppressata slices in a curved line from the top of the board to the bottom, dividing the board like a river.

4. Use the cut gouda and cheddar to make layered lines that border the soppressata, like riverbanks.

5. Put a ramekin of date chutney and a ramekin of honey on either side of the cheese and meat "river."

6. Place the Robiola wheel in one empty corner and stack the manchego triangles in a pile on the other side.

7. Divide the crackers, grapes, prosciutto, and candied nuts into two and use each to fill the gaps on either side of the "river," layering the crackers and scrunching the prosciutto slices into a bouquet.

8. Serve the baguette on the side.

Drink pairing: Pair with pinot grigio, which is adored for its fruity flavors and high acidity. A French style, called pinot gris, will usually be more floral and honeyed, making it a fantastic friend to cheese. If you prefer a more mineral-forward wine with higher acidity, try an Italian pinot grigio.

Cheesemonger wisdom: Gouda originates from Holland, where it was traded in the city of Gouda (pronounced how-da). To make gouda, the cheesemaker pours boiling hot water over the curds, which cooks them and washes the acidity away. Acidity acts as a balance to sweetness, so gouda comes across as a very sweet cheese with notes of butterscotch, caramel, and brown butter. It's typically sealed in wax, which prevents a rind from forming.

TRY IT ALL: HUMBOLDT FOG, MINI BASQUE, PONT L'ÉVÊQUE, STRAVECCHIO, AND CASHEL BLUE

SERVES 8 / ACCOMPANIMENT PREP TIME: 1 HOUR 15 MINUTES

This board has it all: cow, goat, and sheep milk cheeses; bloomy and washed rinds; firm and blue styles; and French, Italian, Irish, American, and Spanish cheeses. Now that you've learned a bit more (or chapters 1 and 2 can remind you), use this plate's diversity to show off your newfound cheese expertise.

½ cup Candied Nuts
(page 101)

¼ cup Apricot
Mustard (page 84)

¼ cup Sun-Dried
Tomato, Caper, and Olive
Tapenade (page 78)

½ wheel (about
10 ounces) Mini Basque

8 ounces Parmigiano-
Reggiano Stravecchio

8 ounces Pont L'Évêque

2 tablespoons honey

½ wheel (about
8 ounces) Humboldt Fog

8 ounces Cashel Blue

2 pears, cut into long,
thin slices

¼ cup cornichons

50 Water Crackers
(page 111) or
store-bought

1. Prepare the candied nuts, and while they're in the oven, prepare the mustard and tapenade.

2. Cut the Mini Basque into small, thin, squat triangles. Crumble the stravecchio into 1-inch pieces. Cut the Pont L'Évêque into small rectangles.

3. Pour the honey into a ramekin and place it in the center of the board. Cut the Humboldt Fog in half and place a wedge on each side of the honey with their tapered points facing each other and their cut sides on the board.

4. Layer the Pont L'Évêque rectangles in one corner of the board. Place the Cashel Blue, wedge upright, in another corner. Pile the stravecchio crumbles off to one side, and line up the Mini Basque triangles in interlocking lines on the other side.

5. Put the mustard (in a ramekin) by the Mini Basque and the tapenade (in a ramekin) by the stravecchio. Fill the gaps on the board with layered pear slices, the cornichons, and candied nuts.

6. Serve the crackers on the side.

continued ›

Try It All *continued*

Drink pairing: With a plate that features so many diverse flavors and textures, it's best to stick with a wine that goes well with cheese more broadly: something with a bit of sweetness, fruit flavors, and good acidity. The classic, of course, is riesling. Try one from the Finger Lakes for an American take on the German noble grape: The Finger Lakes rieslings are full of bright acidity and minerality and might be a bit kinder to your wallet.

Cheesemonger wisdom: Humboldt Fog from California's Cypress Grove Creamery is one of the best-known and -loved American artisan cheeses. Cypress Grove founder Mary Keehn was one of the first cheese pioneers to introduce goat cheese to the American market. Goat cheese was rare stateside before Keehn, and several other women, opened goat cheese-centric creameries in the 1970s and early 1980s.

KEEP IT SIMPLE: MILD BRIE, JARLSBERG, NEW YORK AGED CHEDDAR, AND GRUYÈRE WITH SUMMER SAUSAGE, CORNICHON RELISH, DRIED APRICOTS, AND APPLE BUTTER

SERVES 8 / PREP TIME: 30 MINUTES

Cheese boards don't always need to be fancy, just beautiful and delicious. If you feel like skipping the specialty grocery aisle at the store, here's a casual and approachable board you can put together without compromising on having a stunning composition.

1 8-oz wheel of Brie-style such as Ile de France Brie

½ lb Jarlsberg

½ lb New York Aged White Cheddar

½ lb Gruyère

½ lb Summer Sausage, sliced

⅛ cup of Cornichon and Onion Relish (page 104)

1 cup of dried apricots

¼ cup of Apple Butter (page 88)

½ cup of salted and roasted almonds

50 Water Crackers (page 111) or store-bought

1. Prepare the cornichon relish, up to a few days in advance, and add the relish to a small dish or ramekin and place on each end of the board.

2. Cut the jarlsberg into long thin rectangles, the cheddar into short, thin rectangles, and the Gruyère into long, thin triangles.

3. Arrange the cheddar squares in a layered circle around the apple butter. Arrange the Gruyère triangles in a layered arc around the cornichon ramekin. Arrange the jarlsberg sticks in a layered rectangle in an empty corner of the board. Place the brie in the middle of the board, slightly off-center, with one sample wedge cut out.

4. Layer the summer sausage slices in a curved line, connecting the jarlsberg and brie.

5. Fill in any negative spaces on the board with the nuts and apricots, and water crackers, serving the leftover crackers on the side.

Drink pairing: Drinks with a high alcohol content or strong flavors can overwhelm this board. Try a Belgian witbier, with a citrus fruit finish and subtle spicy notes for just enough flair to pair, but not too much to outshine your carefully curated board.

Cheesemonger Wisdom: When picking out cheeses from a non-specialty section of the grocery store, stay away from pre-shredded, sliced, or crumbled cheeses—they don't stay fresh. Look for European cheeses with the labels AOP, DOP, or PDO; they're name-protected for quality-control. Finally, buy, taste, write down what you like!

MADE IN THE USA: CREMONT, FLORY'S TRUCKLE CHEDDAR, MONTEREY JACK, AND SMOKED GOUDA

SERVES 8 / ACCOMPANIMENT PREP TIME: 2 HOURS

Although Europe might have the longest cheesemaking tradition, don't knock American cheese. Well, it's okay to knock American "cheese" (looking at you, Kraft Singles), but cheesemakers across the United States have perfected cheesemaking and added their own twist. This board celebrates those makers. Prepare this board for your next Independence Day party or when you're just feeling like buying all-American.

¼ cup Tomato Conserve (page 87)

½ cup Candied Nuts (page 101)

8 strips Candied Bacon (page 99), quartered

12 ounces Smoked Gouda

12 ounces Dry Monterey Jack

12 ounces Flory's Truckle Cheddar

1 (5-ounce) wheel Vermont Creamery Cremont

½ cup blueberries

2 apples, thinly sliced

50 Water Crackers (page 111) or store-bought

1. Make the tomato conserve, and while it's simmering, prepare the candied nuts. While the nuts are in the oven, prepare the candied bacon.

2. Put the conserve in a ramekin and place it off-center on the board.

3. Cut the gouda into long, thin triangles; crumble the Monterey Jack into 1-inch chunks; cut the cheddar into small, thin rectangles; and place the whole Cremont in one corner of the board.

4. Surround the conserve ramekin with a ring of Monterey Jack chunks.

5. Outline one edge of the board with a layer the gouda triangles, and do the same with the bacon strips on the interior of the gouda border.

6. Surround the Cremont with the blueberries, and the Monterey Jack chunks with the candied nuts, letting those piles fill out the board. Use the apple slices, layered, to fill up the empty space. If there's any leftover space, fill it with the water crackers, layered, and serve the rest on the side.

Drink pairing: East Coast IPA is wildly different from the traditional bitter IPA. It's very hoppy, but this style of IPA uses different types of hops added at a different part of the brewing process, so the hops add fruity aromas more than bitterness. The beer is usually hazy because it's left unfiltered. These beers are easy drinking; some almost taste like fruit juice and are excellent alongside an American cheddar.

Cheesemonger wisdom: Unlike most styles of cheese, which originated in Europe, Monterey Jack was first made in the United States. David Jack was a Californian entrepreneur who decided to market a mild, white cheese that was being made by Franciscan friars in Monterey, California, in the eighteenth century.

RAINBOW BOARD: VALENÇAY, YOUNG MANCHEGO, TOMA PIEMONTESE, GRUYÈRE, AND SHROPSHIRE BLUE

SERVES 8 / ACCOMPANIMENT PREP TIME: 35 MINUTES

Cheese can have a wide range of color. Bright orange varieties, such as Shropshire Blue or even Kraft Singles, typically have been dyed with a natural plant dye called annatto. Excluding dyes, a cheese's color largely depends on the animal type, its diet, and how long the cheese has been aged. Use these diverse cheese colors—from black and white, to blue and orange, to yellow hues—to build a varied, beautiful board with green, red, and deep purple accompaniments.

¼ cup Wine-Poached Cherries (page 106)

1 (8-ounce) Valençay

10 ounces Young Manchego

8 ounces Toma Piemontese

10 ounces Gruyère

8 ounces speck

1 (8-ounce) wedge Shropshire Blue

1 cup dates

1 cup dried apricots

1 cup salted mixed nuts

¼ cup cornichons

2 baguettes, cut into ¼-inch-thick slices

1. Prepare the cherries.

2. Using a brie knife, cut the Valençay into 8 pieces, making 4 cuts from a bird's-eye view, vertically, horizontally, and on both diagonals. Separate the cut pieces slightly, maintaining the general shape of the cheese, and place it in the center of the board.

3. Cut the manchego into small, squat, thin triangles; the Toma into small, thin rectangles; and the gruyère into long, thin rectangular sticks.

4. Arrange the manchego triangles in two interlocking lines, arched around the Valençay, leaving room between the two cheeses. Fill the space between them with bunched up speck slices.

5. Place the Shropshire Blue wedge in a corner, and place the cherries (in a ramekin) nearby but not touching the wedge. Arrange the toma rectangles in a larger layered rectangle on an empty side of the board, and create a layered line of gruyère triangles where there's the most room.

6. Fill empty areas with the dates, apricots, nuts, and cornichons. Put the cornichons by the gruyère, the dates near the Shropshire, and the apricots by the Toma. Serve the baguette in a bread basket.

Drink pairing: Sangria is a fun way to enjoy wine, and you can make it look gorgeous. Use a base of Spanish white wine, such as Albariño, and layer different colored fruits in each glass for a bright and colorful drink that's as beautiful as it is tasty. Try making a fruit rainbow with layers of blackberries, blueberries, kiwis, pineapple, orange, and strawberries.

Date Night Dessert, page 64

CHAPTER 5

DESSERT BOARDS

DATE NIGHT DESSERT: DOUBLE-CRÈME BRIE, GOLDEN PECORINO, BAYLEY HAZEN BLUE, AND WINE-POACHED CHERRIES

SERVES 4 / ACCOMPANIMENT PREP TIME: 1 HOUR

If you don't already think that cheese is an aphrodisiac, this board will convince you. Indulge in luscious brie, golden pecorino, and a blue that will tantalize your senses. Anyone down for a double date?

¼ cup Wine-Poached Cherries (page 106)

3 tablespoons Chocolate Fig Jam (page 81)

4 strips Candied Bacon (page 99)

5 ounces Pecorino Oro Antico

4 ounces Jasper Hill Bayley Hazen Blue

6 ounces double-crème brie

4 chocolate covered pretzels

¼ cup walnuts

30 to 40 Water Crackers (page 111) or store-bought

1. Prepare the accompaniments: wine-poached cherries, fig jam, and bacon. Cut the bacon strips into quarters.

2. Cut the pecorino into long, thin, rectangular strips. Cut the blue cheese into small triangles.

3. Place the brie wedge in one corner of the board, arrange the pecorino pieces in a layered rectangle in another corner, and layer the blue triangles in a line near the edge of the board farthest from the other two cheeses.

4. Place the cherries (in a ramekin) near the brie, place the fig jam near the blue, and layer the bacon strips near the pecorino.

5. In the center of the board, arrange the pretzels in a circle. Use the walnuts to fill the areas around the pretzels. Serve the crackers on the side.

Drink pairing: Try a cherry-like wine to pair with the wine-poached cherries. Cerasuolo d'Abruzzo—*cerasuolo* means "cherry red" in Italian—is an appropriately named rosé with a deep cherry color and serious fruit flavors, but it's also seriously dry.

Substitution tip: Hearts always make a cute addition to a love themed board. You can use a heart-shaped cookie cutter to make hearts out of a plain fresh chèvre log. If you're crafty, it shouldn't be too hard to form hearts freehand. Mix shredded beets into the chèvre to color the hearts pink!

FRENCH FROMAGE: SAINTE MAURE, LANGRES, COMTÉ, AND FOURME D'AMBERT BLUE WITH SAUCISSON SEC

SERVES 6 / ACCOMPANIMENT PREP TIME: 1 HOUR 15 MINUTES

In France, the cheese course is typically served right before dessert, so it's only natural to serve this all-French board at the end of your meal. Although the French might enjoy dessert after this course, this board alone will satisfy all your after-dinner cravings.

¼ cup candied walnuts (see Candied Nuts on page 101)

1 (8-ounce) log Sainte Maure

8 ounces Comté

8 ounces saucisson sec, cut into thin medallions

1 (6-ounce) wedge Fourme d'Ambert

1 (6-ounce) wheel Langres

2 tablespoons honey

¼ cup strawberries, quartered

¼ cup dried apricots

1½ baguettes, cut into ¼-inch pieces

1. Prepare the candied walnuts.

2. Using a cheese wire, cut half the Sainte Maure log into thin medallions, leaving the other half uncut. In one corner of the board, arrange the slices in front of the log.

3. Cut the comté into long, thin triangles and place them in another corner of the board in a layered line pointing toward the center of the board. Layer the saucisson in a curved line starting from another corner, going toward the center of the board.

4. Put the Fourme d'Ambert wedge in the final corner of the board and put the Langres wheel slightly off-center on the board.

5. Put the honey in a ramekin near the Fourme d'Ambert blue. Fill the nearby area with the strawberries.

6. Encircle the Langres with layered apricots, and fill the rest of the board with the candied walnuts.

7. Serve the baguette in a bread basket.

Drink pairing: Vouvray is a wine region located in France's Loire Valley. All whites from this region are made from the chenin blanc grape and contain notes of honeysuckle, pear, ginger, and apricot. This fantastic wine ranges from a very sweet dessert-style called *moelleux* to dry *sec*. For a real treat, try a demi-sec sparkling Vouvray.

Cheesemonger wisdom: Langres is a cute, wrinkly washed rind with a small depression on the top of the wheel. This little well is there so that you can enjoy Langres according to tradition: by first pouring some marc de champagne or pomace brandy directly on top of the cheese. For festivities, people often pour champagne on top, creating a *fontaine*, or fountain.

NUTTY AND HONEYED CHEESES WITH FARMER'S FRESH SHEEP CHEESE, BOURBON BELLAVITANO, AND BAYLEY HAZEN BLUE

SERVES 5 / ACCOMPANIMENT PREP TIME: 25 MINUTES

Nature has a way of producing the most luxurious foods—no human manipulation needed. This board showcases the naturally rich oils in nuts and the tangy intense sweetness of honey. This dessert plate is literally flowing with (cultured) milk and honey.

¼ cup Lemon Curd (page 86)

8 ounces Bourbon BellaVitano

6 ounces Jasper Hill Bayley Hazen Blue

5 ounces Farmer's Cheese, preferably sheep's milk

2 tablespoons peach preserves

1 small block (about 3 ounces) honeycomb

¼ cup hazelnuts, lightly salted and toasted

¼ cup lightly salted and toasted cashews

1 loaf honey nut bread, cut into crostini-size pieces

1. Prepare the lemon curd.

2. Cut the Bourbon BellaVitano into long, thin triangles, and cut the blue into short, small triangles.

3. Put the farmer's cheese, peach preserves, and lemon curd in separate ramekins and evenly distribute them across the board.

4. Arrange the Bourbon BellaVitano in a layered line starting from the peach preserves. Layer the blue triangles in an empty part of the board and place the honeycomb near it.

5. Fill the empty parts of the board with the hazelnuts and cashews.

6. Serve the bread on the side.

Drink pairing: Madeira is a fortified wine from the eponymous Portuguese island and is known for its rich and nutty characteristics. Madeira Bual is a sweet style that pairs well with hazelnuts and tastes like golden raisins and roasted coffee.

Cheesemonger wisdom: Farmer's cheese is a fresh cheese that comes in a wide variety of forms; it refers to any cheese that farmers make quickly to use up leftover milk. They use cow, goat, or sheep's milk—whatever they have on hand. No matter the milk, it will be mild and creamy with a pronounced tang. If you're lucky enough to find a sheep's milk version, you'll enjoy a decadent richness, but all farmer's cheese is a great treat when paired with fruit jams, nuts, and honey.

CREAM AND CARAMEL WITH TOMME BRÛLÉE, EWEPHORIA AGED GOUDA, AND DANISH BLUE

SERVES 6 / ACCOMPANIMENT PREP TIME: 45 MINUTES

This board is all about the caramel. A caramelized—or brûléed—cheese is cheese's answer to caramel, and aged gouda carries just the right amount of natural caramelized sweetness without any extra brûléeing involved. The salty-rich Danish Blue rounds out the board along with spicy ginger. What else pairs? Well, more caramel, of course!

1 pear from Caramel Pears (page 105), sliced

¼ wheel (7 ounces) Tomme Brûlée

9 ounces Ewephoria Gouda

1 (6-ounce) wedge Danish Blue

¼ cup ginger preserves

1 cup caramel popcorn

¼ cup salted macadamia nuts

30 to 40 salted Water Crackers (page 111) or store-bought

1. Prepare the caramel pears.

2. Cut the top and bottom rinds off the Tomme Brûlée, then slice the partial wheel into even rounded triangles. Cut the gouda into long, thin triangles.

3. Place the Danish Blue wedge on one side of the board. Arrange the Tomme Brûlée wedges in intertwined, zigzagged rows, and create a long row of overlapped gouda triangles down the middle of the board. Place the ginger preserves (in a ramekin) in an empty spot on the board.

4. Arrange the caramel pears in a circle around the ginger ramekin.

5. Fill the gaps on the board with the caramel popcorn and macadamia nuts. Serve the water crackers on the side.

Drink pairing: The perfect splurge, ice wine is made by freezing grapes, which results in a very sugary juice that is made into a sweet wine. This cheese board is already very sweet, but ice wine has more acidity and intense fruit flavors than other dessert wines, making it a more balanced option for this sweet plate.

Cheesemonger wisdom: Cheese is naturally sweet because milk contains natural sugars. When you cook cheese, the sugars caramelize, just as they do when you cook fruit or make homemade caramel. Not all cheeses are cooked, but those that are, such as gouda and Alpines, impart an extra butterscotchy sweetness.

CHOCOLATE AND CHEESE WITH TRIPLE-CRÈME BRIE, BEEMSTER EXTRA AGED GOUDA, STILTON, AND MORE CHOCOLATE

SERVES 6 / ACCOMPANIMENT PREP TIME: 15 MINUTES

Both cheese and chocolate are fermented products, which gives them complex, nuanced flavors as well as acidity, aroma, and tang. A lusciously creamy triple-crème brie works well with velvety and tangy milk chocolates. Aged gouda is nutty and crunchy and forms the perfect bite with a decadent dark truffle. All chocolates are divine with salty and fudgy blue cheeses, but fruity chocolate with stilton is hard to beat. Cheese and chocolate are both sinfully good on their own, and when eaten together, they make a devilishly delicious pair.

3 tablespoons Chocolate Fig Jam (page 81)

8 ounces Stilton

10 ounces Brillat-Savarin, or other triple-crème brie

1 cup strawberries, quartered

9 ounces Beemster Extra Aged Gouda

12 assorted chocolate truffles

½ cup hazelnuts

1 baguette, cut into ¼-inch slices

1. Prepare the fig jam, put it in a ramekin, and place it in one corner of the board.

2. Using a cheese knife, crumble the Stilton into 1-inch pieces and surround the fig jam with the blue crumbles.

3. Place the Brillat-Savarin opposite the Stilton. Arrange the strawberries around the triple-crème.

4. Cut the gouda into long, thin rectangles and arrange them into a layered rectangle spanning the center of the board.

5. Outline the gouda rectangle with the chocolate truffles.

6. Fill the gaps with the hazelnuts.

7. Serve with the baguette slices.

Drink pairing: The only thing that might be as sexy as cheese and chocolate is red wine and chocolate. Try Amarone della Valpolicella, an Italian red made from dried grapes, primarily the corvina grape. Amarone is full-bodied and intense with a velvety texture and flavors of cherry liquor, dried fig, and, of course, chocolate.

Cheesemonger wisdom: Stilton is one of the best known British cheeses and has earned European name protected status. Stilton must be made from local and pasteurized cow's milk in the three counties of Derbyshire, Leicestershire, and Nottinghamshire. The result is a rich and mellow blue that tastes of earth, grass, and butter with beautiful blue veins and a fudgy texture.

I LOVE BLUE: CHOCOLATE FIG JAM, APPLE BUTTER, HONEY, AND CANDIED PECANS

SERVES 4 / ACCOMPANIMENT PREP TIME: 2 HOURS 25 MINUTES

This board showcases the great range of blue cheeses, from Cambozola and fudgy, orange-dyed Shropshire to sweet Gorgonzola to peppery and fierce Roquefort. The intense flavors of blue cheese can overwhelm your palate, making it hard to enjoy everything that comes afterward, so be sure to end your evening with this all-blue treat.

3 tablespoons Apple Butter (page 88)

¼ cup candied pecans (see Candied Nuts on page 101)

3 tablespoons Chocolate Fig Jam (page 81)

3 tablespoons honey

6 ounces Cambozola Black Label

6 ounces Shropshire Blue

6 ounces Roquefort

1 (6-ounce) wedge Gorgonzola Dolce

1 pear, thinly sliced

1 baguette, cut into ¼-inch slices

1. Prepare the apple butter, and while it is simmering, prepare the candied pecans and fig jam. Put the fig jam, apple butter, and honey in separate ramekins. Place the apple butter ramekin near the corner of a rectangular board, or on the edge of a round board.

2. Using a cheese wire, cut the Cambozola into small, squat rectangles. Cut the Shropshire into thin triangles. Crumble the Roquefort into 1-inch pieces. Leave the Gorgonzola wedge whole.

3. In the center of the board, arrange the Shropshire triangles in a layered line, somewhat dividing the board into two. Curve the end of the line slightly around the apple butter ramekin.

4. In one corner of the board, arrange the Cambozola rectangles in a layered arch. Place the honey ramekin in the center of the arch.

5. Place the fig jam ramekin catty-corner from the cambozola and pile the crumbled Roquefort around the side, facing the center of the board.

6. In the space farthest from the other cheeses, place the Gorgonzola, and layer the pear slices nearby.

7. Fill the gaps on the board with the candied pecans. Serve the baguette in a basket.

Drink pairing: Sauternes is a French dessert wine that pairs exceptionally well with Roquefort. Sauternes is made from late-harvest grapes that have been affected by noble rot, which gives it its characteristic honeyed sweetness.

Cheesemonger wisdom: Although blue mold is what makes blue cheese tasty, the cheese was sold at its optimum blue growth, so you don't want to encourage more. Keep your blue cheese wrapped in aluminum foil to limit blue mold growth.

MUSHROOM MANIA: BRIE, FONTINA VAL D'AOSTA, TRUFFLE PECORINO, BRESAOLA, AND MUSHROOM SPREAD

SERVES 6 / ACCOMPANIMENT PREP TIME: 55 MINUTES

The rich, musky, and earthy taste of mushrooms can be intense but is absolutely divine when paired correctly. Certain cheeses mirror the natural robust and lusty qualities of mushrooms, such as the funky flavors in brie or the silky texture of Fontina Val d'Aosta. Some cheesemakers play up the mushroominess of cheese by adding seductive truffle to it, like this board's pecorino, which goes well with a meaty and musty cured bresaola.

3 tablespoons Sweet and Tangy Sautéed Shallots (page 98)

¼ cup Truffled Mushroom Spread (page 79)

8 ounces Fontina Val d'Aosta

10 ounces Truffle Pecorino

1 (8-ounce) wheel brie-style cheese

8 ounces bresaola, thinly sliced

2 ounces dark chocolate, broken into squares

¼ cup walnuts

3 thyme sprigs

30 to 40 Water Crackers (page 111) or store-bought

1. Prepare the shallots, and while the shallots simmer, prepare the mushroom spread. Put the shallots and spread in separate ramekins. Place the mushroom ramekin in the center of the board.

2. Cut the fontina into long, thin triangles, and cut the pecorino into small, thin rectangles.

3. Place the brie wheel in a corner of the board and cut one wedge, leaving it in place.

4. Starting at another corner of the board, arrange the fontina triangles in a layered line pointing inward. Arrange the pecorino squares in a large, layered rectangle in another corner.

5. Put the shallot ramekin near the brie, on the inner side of the cheese.

6. Loosely fold the bresaola slices into quarters and place them together in the center of the board, around the mushroom spread.

7. Pile the chocolate squares on an empty part of the board, close to the pecorino but not touching.

8. Pile the walnuts in two or three places to fill large gaps on the board. Place 2 thyme sprigs directly on the brie and the third sprig near the mushroom spread.

9. If there's room on one edge of the board, fill it with layered water crackers, or serve them on the side.

Drink pairing: Red Burgundy is velvety, rich, and classic enough for this earthy and extravagant plate. Flavors of earth, dust, and must call for a robust and earthy pinot noir from Burgundy. Look for wines from the Burgundy subregion of Côte de Nuits (referring to walnut trees), which are known for full-bodied pinot noirs with notes of fresh red fruits and earthy mushrooms.

Cheesemonger wisdom: There's science behind the mushroomy flavors in both cheese and wine. There's a chemical called mushroom alcohol (1-octen-3-ol, or octenol for short) that's produced by the white mold that gives brie its bloomy rind. Mushroom alcohol is found in wine and other cheeses that have characteristic musty, earthy, and rustic notes.

CREAM AND COFFEE WITH RICOTTA, GOUDA ROOMANO, ESPRESSO BELLAVITANO, BARELY BUZZED, AND COFFEE BUTTER

SERVES 5 / ACCOMPANIMENT PREP TIME: 1 HOUR 10 MINUTES

Cheese and coffee as dessert is by no means a new idea: Tiramisu is essentially fresh triple crème (mascarpone) and espresso. These coffee-rubbed cheeses, with flavors of butterscotch and rich cream, are the perfect pick-me-up. This coffee-oriented board works just as well for brunch as it does in place of or alongside your after-dinner coffee.

¼ cup Maple-Cayenne Glazed Nuts (page 100), divided

4 tablespoons Coffee Butter (page 89)

¼ cup orange marmalade

6 ounces Fresh Ricotta

5 shortbread cookies

6 ounces Gouda Roomano

6 ounces espresso BellaVitano

6 ounces Beehive Barely Buzzed

¼ cup blueberries

25 to 35 Water Crackers (page 111) or store-bought

1. Prepare the maple-cayenne nuts and coffee butter. Put the coffee butter and orange marmalade in separate ramekins.

2. Put the ricotta in a ramekin and place it toward one corner of the board. Fan the shortbread cookies around one side of the ricotta ramekin. Surround the other side with half of the maple-cayenne nuts.

3. Cut the gouda into long, thin sticks; cut the espresso BellaVitano into long, thin triangles; and slice the Barely Buzzed into short, squat triangles.

4. Arrange the Barely Buzzed triangles so that they are upright, and make a curved line with them in the center of the board.

5. Place the ramekin of coffee butter next to the Barely Buzzed triangles. Surround the ramekin with the rest of the maple-cayenne nuts.

6. In a corner of the board, layer the gouda sticks in a rectangle.

7. Place the ramekin of marmalade in another corner, and fan out the BellaVitano triangles so that the short ends of the triangles are touching the marmalade ramekin.

8. Fill the rest of the board with the blueberries and serve with the water crackers.

Drink pairing: Stouts are made with roasted malts, which give them chocolatey flavors and notes of roasted coffee and is why so many brewers put actual coffee into the beer itself. Coffee goes particularly well with a dark beer, such as a porter or stout. Try Stone's Coffee Milk Stout, AleSmith's Speedway Stout, and Founders' Breakfast Stout. Or skip the alcohol altogether and have a cup of joe with these cheeses.

Beet Jam with Rosemary, Thyme, and Honey, page 76

CHAPTER 6

DIPS, SPREADS, AND JAMS

BEET JAM WITH ROSEMARY, THYME, AND HONEY

MAKES 2 PINTS / PREP TIME: 20 MINUTES / COOK TIME: 1 HOUR

Beets are magical because they're deeply earthy but balanced with natural sweetness. They are so intensely bright pink it's hard to believe their color is natural; just be careful not to dye your kitchen pink! The vibrant hue looks beautiful next to snow-white fresh chèvre, and the pair taste great together, too.

4 large red beets

2 teaspoons salt

3 thyme sprigs

3 rosemary sprigs

3 tablespoons honey

Juice of 1 lemon

1. Put the beets in a large saucepan over high heat and cover with 1 to 2 inches of water. Add the salt.

2. Bring the water to a rolling boil, cover the pan with a lid, and reduce the heat to low.

3. Simmer for 30 to 45 minutes, depending on the size of the beets, until the beets are tender when pierced with a fork.

4. Remove beets the from the water, and while they're still hot but cool enough to handle, use a paper towel to remove and discard the skins.

5. Coarsely chop the beets into large chunks and puree them in a blender. Transfer the puree to the saucepan.

6. Using kitchen twine, tie the thyme and rosemary together.

7. Add the herbs, honey, and lemon juice to the puree and bring it to a simmer over low heat.

8. Simmer for 30 minutes, stirring occasionally to ensure the bottom of the puree doesn't burn.

9. Using a large fork or tongs, remove the herbs and transfer the jam to jars. Follow proper canning technique to seal the jars and keep them for up to 3 months. Otherwise, store the jam in the refrigerator for up to 4 days.

Substitution tip: If the flavor of red beets reminds you too much of soil, or if you're worried about accidentally dying everything bright pink, opt for golden beets. Golden beets have a beautiful bright yellow color, are slightly sweeter, and have a less concentrated earthy flavor than red beets.

SUN-DRIED TOMATO, CAPER, AND OLIVE TAPENADE

MAKES ABOUT 1½ CUPS / PREP TIME: 5 MINUTES

Traditional Mediterranean tapenade is made with minced olives and anchovies and can be eaten with many foods: as a spread on crostini, with seared tuna, or on Provençal-style chicken. But tapenade is best with cheese because of its salty, oily, and acidic character. Try this tapenade with Asiago or a buttery sheep's milk cheese, such as manchego. This version skips the anchovies for a vegetarian approach and uses sun-dried tomatoes to balance the salt and tartness with a touch of sweetness.

¾ cup sun-dried tomatoes

1 cup kalamata olives, pitted

2 garlic cloves

2 tablespoons extra-virgin olive oil

3 tablespoons capers, drained

1 tablespoon red wine vinegar

1 teaspoon red pepper flakes (optional)

Salt

Freshly ground black pepper

1. Combine the tomatoes, olives, garlic, oil, capers, vinegar, and red pepper flakes (if using) in a food processor and pulse until coarsely chopped.

2. Add salt and pepper to taste.

Substitution tip: If you want to bring in extra sweetness, you can add three tablespoons of my chopped Roasted Red Peppers (page 103) or even completely substitute the sun-dried tomatoes with Roasted Red Peppers.

TRUFFLED MUSHROOM SPREAD

MAKES 2 CUPS / PREP TIME: 10 MINUTES / COOK TIME: 20 MINUTES

Mushrooms have a robust, meaty quality that allows you to make a pâté-like spread without any meat. Mushroom spread pairs especially well with earthy cheeses, such as funky camembert and brie, as well as oily and rich cheeses, such as aged pecorino. Truffle oil is super pungent and is used sparingly for some delightful decadence.

⅓ pound cremini mushrooms

⅓ pound shiitake mushrooms

⅓ pound porcini mushrooms

2 tablespoons extra-virgin olive oil

1 large shallot, chopped

2 garlic cloves, minced

1 tablespoon white truffle oil

2 tablespoons dry white wine

Salt

Freshly ground black pepper

1. Remove the stems from the cremini, shiitake, and porcini mushrooms and coarsely chop them. Set aside.

2. Heat the olive oil in a large saucepan over medium-high heat. Add the shallot and cook for 3 to 5 minutes, until tender.

3. Add the chopped mushrooms, garlic, and truffle oil and cook for another 6 minutes, until the mushrooms are soft and the garlic is golden.

4. Add the wine and cook for another 2 to 5 minutes, until the liquid has reduced by half.

5. Transfer the mixture to a food processor and pulse until well minced and combined but not quite smooth.

6. Add salt and pepper to taste.

Substitution tip: There are dozens of types of mushroom. Mildly meaty cremini, deeply nutty shiitake, and rich woodsy porcini are used here, but add or substitute other kinds for different flavor profiles. For a milder spread, use fewer shiitake and porcini and add white button mushrooms, or try adding chanterelles for their creamy richness.

HAZELNUT AGRODOLCE

MAKES ABOUT 2 CUPS / PREP TIME: 15 MINUTES / COOK TIME: 25 MINUTES

Agrodolce might be the most underrated cheese accompaniment. It's an Italian sauce that incorporates sweet and sour flavors (*agro* meaning sour, and *dolce* meaning sweet) and is made by reducing sugar and vinegar. It should be no surprise that something tart and sweet balances out a creamy and salty cheese, such as Comté. This version uses sweet and elegant hazelnuts to highlight the natural nuttiness in cheese and provide texture.

¼ cup raisins

1 cup water

2 tablespoons extra-virgin olive oil

1 cup hazelnuts, roughly chopped

⅓ cup honey

1 cup red wine vinegar

1. Soak the raisins in the water for about 10 minutes, until plump, and then drain.

2. Heat the olive oil in a small skillet over medium heat. Lightly toast the hazelnuts, tossing them frequently for about 4 minutes, until they are fragrant and lightly golden. Transfer them to a bowl and let cool.

3. Heat a small saucepan over low heat. Pour in the honey and vinegar and stir to combine. Bring to a simmer and cook for 15 to 20 minutes, until thickened.

4. Allow the honey-vinegar mixture to cool. Add the hazelnuts and raisins and stir to combine.

5. The agrodolce can be stored in the refrigerator for up to 5 days.

Cooking tip: Use any leftovers as a sauce with roasted meats or vegetables that could benefit from a little sweetness and texture, such as pork chops or acorn squash. Alternatively, temper a super sweet dessert—creamy cheesecake, for example—with a bit of acidity.

CHOCOLATE FIG JAM

MAKES ABOUT 1½ CUPS / PREP TIME: 5 MINUTES / COOK TIME: 10 MINUTES

Homemade jams and preserves have a wonderful depth of flavor, but they can take a long time to make. This recipe uses dried figs to give the same richness of flavor in half the time. The honey and raisin flavors of Mission figs go perfectly with dark chocolate for a not-too-sweet dessert pairing.

6 ounces (about 22) dried Mission figs, stems removed, chopped

1 cup sugar

1 cup water

Juice of 1 lemon

2 tablespoons baking cocoa

1 teaspoon vanilla extract

1. Combine all the ingredients in a medium saucepan over medium-high heat and bring to a boil.

2. Reduce the heat to low and simmer for 8 to 10 minutes, until the figs are soft and the liquid has become slightly thickened and viscous. Remove the pan from the heat and let cool for 5 minutes.

3. Transfer the mixture to a blender and puree until almost smooth.

4. Let cool. Store in the refrigerator for up to 5 days, or seal with proper canning technique to store for up to 3 months.

Food pairing: Figs and chocolate are both classic blue cheese pairings, bringing out the cheese style's natural fruity and fudgy flavors. But the uses don't stop there. My Chocolate Fig Jam is delicious served on pancakes or used as the jelly in a PB&J because peanut butter and chocolate is divine.

FALL SPICE INFUSED HONEY

MAKE-AHEAD / MAKES 2 CUPS / PREP TIME: 5 MINUTES, PLUS 5 DAYS FOR INFUSION

Infused honey is an amazingly versatile condiment. If, somehow, it doesn't all get eaten alongside your cheese board, you can add this honey to tea or cocktails or use it to make mulled wine. Or, spread it on toast in the morning. For more intensity of flavor, let the honey infuse longer in the jar, for up to two weeks.

3 tablespoons
whole cloves

3 cinnamon sticks

1 teaspoon star anise

1 tablespoon whole
allspice

15 ounces honey

1. Put the cloves, cinnamon sticks, star anise, and allspice into a 16-ounce glass jar.

2. Pour the honey on top until the jar is full, and seal the jar.

3. Store the jar in a cool, dry place for at least 5 days. Store it longer (up to 2 weeks) for a more intense flavor, but taste it along the way, so you can stop the infusion before the flavor is too concentrated.

4. Strain the honey through a colander to remove the spices and enjoy.

Substitution tip: You can infuse honey with nearly any of your favorite spices and flavors. A few possibilities are whole coffee beans, dried lavender, and vanilla bean. Use one to two tablespoons of dried spices per cup of honey, but use less for stronger flavors, such as star anise.

HOT PEPPER HONEY

MAKES 2 CUPS / PREP TIME: 5 MINUTES / COOK TIME: 1 HOUR

Hot pepper honey is a great way to enjoy a bit of heat with your sweet. Cheese can handle a little spice because the cream helps cool things down. This recipe uses Calabrian chiles, a small red pepper from the "toe" of Italy. These peppers really pack a punch, so if you want a milder heat, either reduce the cook time of this recipe or opt for a milder pepper, such as Fresno chiles.

4 Calabrian chiles

2 cups honey

1. Using gloves, destem and deseed the chiles.

2. In a saucepan over low heat, combine the honey and chiles and simmer for 1 hour, tasting occasionally. Once you've reached your desired level of heat, strain the honey through a sieve into a jar.

3. Let cool and store in the jar for up to 1 week in the refrigerator or up to 3 months if you seal the jar with proper canning technique (see page 85).

Cooking tip: You'll probably want to make lots of this hot pepper honey because it's so versatile and delicious. To increase the volume, just add two chiles for every cup of honey. You can drizzle the extra honey over fried chicken, biscuits, ice cream, or even pizza.

APRICOT MUSTARD

MAKES 2 CUPS / PREP TIME: 5 MINUTES / COOK TIME: 45 MINUTES

Mustard's distinctive bite blends surprisingly well with the sweetness of apricot jam. The Dijon mustard brings out the horseradish-like flavors found in aged cheddar, while the fruit adds balance. This brilliantly orange condiment has so much going on that you'll be shocked to know that making it is as simple as mixing Dijon mustard and apricot jam! And if you're in a real rush, you can buy both those ingredients at the store and blend them together in a one-to-one ratio.

¾ cup fresh apricots, peeled, pitted, and chopped

3 tablespoons water

½ cup sugar

1 teaspoon freshly squeezed lemon juice

1 cup Dijon mustard

1. In a medium saucepan over medium-high heat, combine the apricots and water and bring it to a boil, then reduce the heat to low and simmer for about 10 minutes, stirring constantly.

2. When the apricots are mushy, add the sugar and lemon juice, increase the heat to medium high, and bring the mixture to a gentle boil.

3. Cook for about 30 minutes, stirring occasionally to make sure the bottom doesn't burn, and skimming off any foam that forms.

4. When the apricots are completely mashed and the consistency of the jam has thickened, remove it from the heat and let cool.

5. Once cooled, transfer 1 cup of the jam to a blender and blend with the mustard (see this recipe's cooking tip for how to use the remaining jam).

6. Store in a jar in the refrigerator for up to 5 days, or can according to proper canning technique (see page 85) to store it for up to 6 months.

Cooking tip: This recipe will yield a little more than 1 cup of apricot jam. You can separately can the apricot jam or store it separately in the refrigerator for up to 5 days. Spread the jam on toast with cottage cheese or enjoy it with an herbed scone and tea.

CANNING AT HOME

Home canning is remarkably easy, and you really don't need anything other than canning jars, a large pot, and water. If you've gone to the trouble of making a delicious accompaniment, it's smart to can the leftovers for later use. Homemade canned goods also make great gifts. Here are the easy steps to canning effectively at home.

First, sterilize your jars. Wash the jars and lids with dish soap and place the jars (not the lids) right-side up on a wire rack in a deep saucepot. Pour water into the saucepot so that the water covers the jars by about two inches and bring it to a boil. Boil the jars for 10 minutes. If the can contents are not yet ready, keep the jars in the water but reduce the heat to a simmer to keep everything warm.

When you're ready to fill the jars, remove them from the saucepot. Spoon or pour the accompaniment or dip into the jars, wipe away any food on the outside, place the lids on top, and seal them tightly with the metal bands. Place the jars back into the saucepot and cover them with two to three inches of water. Bring the water to a boil. Smaller jars must be boiled for at least 10 minutes, whereas 16-ounce jars need at least 15 minutes of boiling time to achieve a seal. Turn the heat off and let the jars cool in the pot for another 10 minutes before removing them with tongs. To check if you've achieved a seal, press down on the center of the lid. If the lid doesn't pop back up, you're good to go.

This canning method is best suited to highly acidic foods. For further instruction on what you're able to can, and to be sure that you're always practicing food safety, refer to the USDA's *Complete Guide to Home Canning*.

LEMON CURD

You might primarily think of lemon curd as an ingredient in baked goods, such as lemon bars or lemon tarts, but it's quite delicious alongside cheese. The thickened texture of the curd gives it a creamy body to match any cheese, and the sunny brightness is especially delicious with goat cheeses.

1 (4-ounce) stick butter, at room temperature

¾ cup sugar

Juice and zest of 3 large lemons

⅛ teaspoon salt

4 egg yolks

1. In a small bowl, cream the butter and sugar together.

2. Heat a small saucepan over low heat. Transfer the butter mixture to the pan and cook until the butter has melted, then add the lemon juice, zest, and salt. Whisk in the egg yolks, one at a time, combining each yolk fully before adding the next.

3. Continue to cook over low heat for about 10 minutes, until the curd has thickened and coats the back of a metal spoon.

4. Let cool at room temperature for at least 5 minutes, and then transfer it to the refrigerator to cool for at least another 10 minutes to develop a thicker consistency.

Cooking tip: The lemon zest adds a little texture and tempers some of the sweetness, but if you prefer a totally smooth curd, you can skip it. Make extra curd to use as filling for a lemon tart, dollop on top of ice cream, or add as a layer to a fruit parfait.

TOMATO CONSERVE

MAKES 1 PINT / PREP TIME: 5 MINUTES / COOK TIME: 1 TO 2 HOURS

Tomatoes represent the best of summer: juicy, bright, and sweet, all in abundance. For the most flavor, make sure to get really ripe tomatoes. Tomatoes already straddle the line between savory and sweet, and this conserve brings out both. If you like an extra kick, add more cayenne pepper.

1½ pounds ripe Roma tomatoes, cored and chopped

1 cup sugar

2 tablespoons freshly squeezed lemon juice

1 teaspoon grated fresh ginger

1 teaspoon salt

1 teaspoon cayenne pepper

½ teaspoon ground cumin

½ teaspoon smoked paprika

1. Combine all the ingredients in a heavy saucepan or Dutch oven over medium-high heat and bring to a boil, stirring often.

2. Reduce the heat to medium and gently boil for 1 to 2 hours, stirring occasionally, until the mixture has thickened to the consistency of jam.

3. Let cool and store it in a jar in the refrigerator for up to 2 weeks, or follow proper canning instructions (see page 85) and store it for up to 1 year.

Ingredient tip: Use leftover Tomato Conserve by baking it into tartlets topped with crumbled feta or whisking it into a vinaigrette. It's also a great finishing touch to dollop on deviled eggs or avocado toast.

APPLE BUTTER

MAKES 2 TO 3 PINTS / PREP TIME: 5 MINUTES / COOK TIME: 2 HOURS 20 MINUTES

There's no real butter or dairy of any sort in apple butter; it's called that because of its thick, creamy texture that spreads like butter. Apple butter will transform any cheese board into a fall treat. Try it with cheddar and blue cheeses, or just spread it over a baguette and crumble the cheese on top for an autumn breakfast.

10 to 12 (about
4 pounds) Gala apples,
peeled, cored, chopped

1 cup light brown sugar

1 teaspoon
vanilla extract

1 tablespoon ground
cinnamon

Juice and zest
of 1 lemon

½ teaspoon
ground cloves

¼ teaspoon
ground nutmeg

¼ teaspoon salt

1. In a large saucepan or Dutch oven over medium heat, combine all the ingredients and cook for about 20 minutes, stirring regularly, until the apples are soft.

2. Puree the mixture with an immersion blender, or transfer it in batches to a stand blender to puree all the ingredients. Return the puree to the saucepan.

3. Reduce the heat to medium-low and cook for about 2 hours, stirring occasionally so the bottom doesn't burn, until the mixture is a medium-dark brown color and the consistency has thickened.

4. Let cool and store it in the refrigerator for about 1 week, or follow proper canning instructions (see page 85) and store for up to 3 months.

Substitution tip: You can use a variety of apples for this recipe. Although Granny Smith apples are popular in baking, they aren't ideal and can result in a tart butter. In addition to Gala, try Fuji and Red Delicious. Be sure to taste a small bite of your apples—some naturally have more sugar than others—so you can adjust the amount of sugar you add.

COFFEE BUTTER

MAKES 1 CUP / PREP TIME: 5 MINUTES / COOK TIME: 30 MINUTES

You may have heard of butter coffee: the popular trend of putting butter directly into hot coffee. This isn't quite that; it's coffee butter—that is, butter flavored with coffee. You'll need to use espresso powder instead of coffee to get enough strength of flavor for the butter and a little salt to balance out the bitterness.

2 tablespoons espresso powder

2½ cups water

2 (4-ounce) sticks unsalted butter, at room temperature

¼ cup confectioner's sugar

¼ teaspoon kosher salt

1. In a small saucepan over medium-high heat, combine the espresso powder and water and bring to a boil, whisking to combine.

2. Remove the saucepan from the stove and let cool to drinking temperature. You can put it in the refrigerator to speed up the cooling.

3. In a large mixing bowl or the bowl of a stand blender, cream the butter, confectioner's sugar, and salt together until fully combined.

4. With the blender on high, pour the espresso liquid into the bowl in small quantities, stopping to scrape the sides of the bowl and fully combine. It's okay if there's a small amount of espresso left uncombined in the bowl (a tablespoon or two at most) after carefully adding and scraping.

5. Scrape the butter from the bowl and transfer it to a small bowl or ramekin. Serve immediately, or chill in the refrigerator for up to 1 week.

Cooking tip: If you're looking for an easy but delicious breakfast, try this butter spread over warm biscuits, and then crumble a sweet cheese, such as aged gouda, on top. The firm texture and crunchy crystals in the cheese are balanced by the smooth butter, while the cheese's candy-like quality is a match for the coffee's bitterness.

DATE CHUTNEY

MAKES ABOUT 1½ CUPS / PREP TIME: 10 MINUTES / COOK TIME: 10 MINUTES

Chutney is wonderful because it's adaptable, but at its core, it is somewhere between a relish and a jam, and it has a great chunky texture and deep flavors. Chutneys balance sweet and sour, though some tend toward one end of the spectrum, such as this date chutney, which is on the sweeter side. This chutney pairs beautifully with salty cheeses, such as blues and pecorinos.

2 tablespoons
vegetable oil

½ cup chopped shallots

1 cup dates, pitted
and chopped

½ cup water

¼ cup apple
cider vinegar

¼ cup light brown sugar

½ cup raisins

1 tablespoon grated
fresh ginger

1 teaspoon red
pepper flakes

1 teaspoon ground
cardamom

1. Heat the oil in a sauté pan or skillet over medium-high heat. Add the shallots and cook for about 3 minutes, until soft and lightly golden.

2. Add the remaining ingredients and bring the mixture to a boil. Then, reduce the heat to low and simmer for about 7 minutes, stirring occasionally, until thickened.

3. Let cool. Store the chutney in the refrigerator for up to 3 weeks.

Substitution tip: Swap out the dates with another fruit for a very different flavor profile to pair with different cheeses. An apple base (try Granny Smith) will go wonderfully with farmhouse cheddar, and a peach base will be delicious alongside a semisoft rustic tomme.

WHOLE-GRAIN BEER MUSTARD

MAKE-AHEAD / MAKES 2 TO 3 CUPS / PREP TIME: 5 MINUTES, PLUS 3 DAYS REFRIGERATION

What do you serve with German sausages, soft pretzels, and a cheese board fit for a brewer? Beer and mustard. This recipe makes it easy for you by putting them together. The beer adds an extra punch of flavor, and leaving the mustard seeds whole adds a pop of texture. Yellow mustard seeds are milder than brown, so a mixture gives a medium spice level (and a pretty color), but feel free to alter the balance based on your preferences.

½ cup brown
mustard seeds

½ cup yellow
mustard seeds

¾ cup apple
cider vinegar

¾ cup beer of your
choice with balanced
malt and hop

½ teaspoon ground
turmeric

2 tablespoons
brown sugar

2 teaspoons salt

1. In a medium bowl, mix together the brown and yellow mustard seeds. Add the apple cider vinegar and beer and stir, then cover and refrigerate for at least 12 hours, preferably 24, until the seeds have absorbed the liquid.

2. Add the turmeric, brown sugar, and salt.

3. Pour the mixture into a food processor and pulse for 30 seconds to 1 minute to achieve your desired grainy texture.

4. Transfer the mustard to jars and cover them with lids. Refrigerate for at least 2 days before use to let the mustard develop flavor. The mustard will last in the refrigerator for 5 months, but the longer it sits, the spicier the flavor will be.

Substitution tip: Although you can use any beer, I recommend a beer with enough flavor to stand up to the pungent mustard seeds and enough malt sweetness to add a little contrast to any mustardy bitterness. Try an amber ale, brown ale, extra special bitter, or doppelbock. For a bit more intensity of flavor, opt for a porter or stout. IPAs might overwhelm the already bitter condiment, and a pale ale or lager may simply get lost.

GREEN OLIVE PESTO

MAKES ABOUT 1½ CUPS / PREP TIME: 10 MINUTES / COOK TIME: 10 MINUTES

Pesto is one of the most versatile sauces because any of its ingredients can be replaced with a similar one, and it's still recognizably pesto. Traditional pesto uses olive oil, pine nuts, basil, Parmigiano-Reggiano, salt, and crushed garlic, but you can substitute any oil, nut, or green and even add some ingredients. This recipe uses walnuts instead of pine nuts and adds green olives for a briny, tangy take.

⅓ cup walnuts, chopped

1 cup green olives, pitted, drained, and packed

2 garlic cloves, minced

½ cup packed fresh basil leaves

¼ cup freshly grated Parmigiano-Reggiano

⅓ cup extra-virgin olive oil

1. Preheat the oven to 350°F. Arrange the walnuts in a single layer on a baking sheet and toast for 5 to 10 minutes, until golden-brown. Be sure to check them often so they don't burn. Let the walnuts cool.

2. Combine the olives, garlic, basil, and cheese in a food processor. Add the cooled walnuts.

3. Turn the food processor on to puree, and drizzle in the olive oil while the ingredients combine. Continue to add oil until you achieve a sauce-like consistency.

4. The pesto can be kept in the refrigerator for about 1 week.

Food pairing: This pesto is delicious with a firm pecorino. The buttery, oily flavors of the sheep's milk pair with the unctuousness of the olive pesto. You can also dollop it on burrata or fresh mozzarella di bufala for an Italian dream.

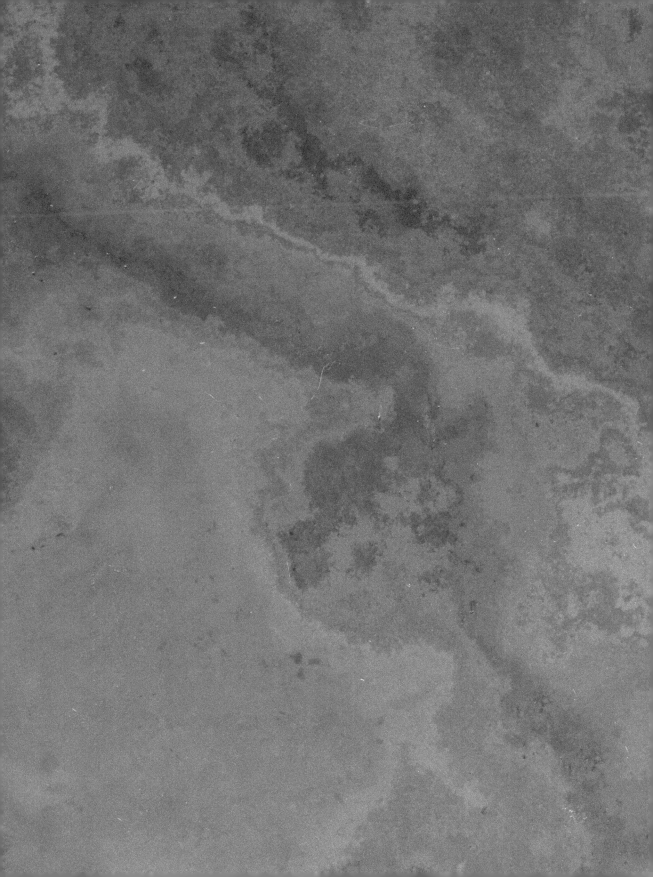

Dried Blood Oranges, page 109

CHAPTER 7

FLAVORFUL ACCOMPANIMENTS

TARRAGON-CHAMPAGNE PICKLED STRAWBERRIES

MAKES ABOUT 1½ CUPS / PREP TIME: 10 MINUTES / COOK TIME: 10 MINUTES

Pickled vegetables, such as cucumbers and string beans, might be more classic, but pickling fruit is just as delicious. It's a great way to dial down what can be overwhelming sweetness and highlight natural tartness. This recipe is a quick pickle, meaning that it uses vinegar as the primary souring agent rather than fermentation, so you'll have to enjoy it within a month or two, but that shouldn't be a problem with these refined, complex, but easily made pickled strawberries.

¾ pound
strawberries, diced

2 tarragon sprigs

6 tablespoons
champagne vinegar

1 tablespoon sugar

1 tablespoon salt

3 tablespoons water

1. Put the diced strawberries in a heatproof jar, along with the tarragon.

2. In a medium saucepan over medium heat, bring the vinegar, sugar, salt, and water to a simmer for about 2 minutes, stirring to ensure that the sugar and salt dissolve. Once dissolved, increase the heat to high and bring to a boil.

3. When the mixture is boiling, pour the liquid over the strawberries and tarragon in the jar. Let cool, and then serve immediately, or refrigerate for at least 24 hours for the most flavor. Keep it in the refrigerator for up to 2 weeks, or follow proper canning technique (see page 85) to store it for at least 3 months.

Substitution tip: Tarragon is a subtle but distinctive herb often used in French cooking, particularly in delicate dressings and sauces, making it a lovely addition to pickled strawberries. Try substituting sweet basil for a more fragrant and stronger flavor.

PICKLED FENNEL

MAKE-AHEAD / MAKES 1 QUART / PREP TIME: 10 MINUTES / COOK TIME: 10 MINUTES,
PLUS 24 HOURS REFRIGERATION

Fennel is a beautiful bulb, and although the fronds taste like anise, the bulb is mild and sweet with a nice oniony crunch. This recipe includes fennel seeds to add that licorice-like flavor, but some people don't enjoy it, so feel free to omit them if you prefer. Pickled fennel won't overpower any cheese but rather adds an herbaceous note and will definitely stand out on any board as something a little different from your standard pickle.

½ teaspoon fennel seeds (optional)

2 fennel bulbs, thinly sliced

Zest of 1 orange

2 garlic cloves, smashed

1 teaspoon peppercorns

1 cup white wine vinegar

½ cup water

2 tablespoons sugar

2 tablespoons kosher salt

1. Toast the fennel seeds (if using) in a pan over medium-high heat for about 2 minutes, until fragrant and slightly browned.

2. In a jar, combine the fennel slices, toasted fennel seeds (if using), orange zest, peppercorns, and garlic and tightly pack the ingredients into a quart-size jar, leaving a ¾-inch space at the top.

3. In a saucepan over medium-high heat, combine the vinegar, water, sugar, and salt and bring to a boil. Stir to dissolve the salt and sugar, and then pour the brine into the jar over the fennel mixture.

4. Tap the jar as needed to remove air bubbles. Fill it to the top with the remaining brine and seal the jar with the lid.

5. Let cool and refrigerate at least overnight before use. Use within 5 days.

Cooking tip: Good pickles will retain a crunch. Fennel bulb is naturally firm, making it a great pickling candidate, but to ensure that satisfying crunchy texture, be sure to pick the freshest bulb. Look for bright white skin without brown spots or abrasions.

SWEET AND TANGY SAUTÉED SHALLOTS

MAKES ABOUT 1½ CUPS / PREP TIME: 10 MINUTES / COOK TIME: 45 MINUTES

Shallots have the sweet, acidic, tangy, and spicy qualities of other onions but are much more delicate and have a slight garlicky note. They sweeten up more when sautéed, so adding vinegar balances the caramelized sugars. This recipe allows you to appreciate all the delicate flavors of shallots and will add some texture to your cheese board.

2 tablespoons
extra-virgin olive oil

1 pound (8 or 9 medium)
shallots, thinly sliced

2 tablespoons sugar

2 thyme sprigs

2 rosemary sprigs

3 tablespoons
balsamic vinegar

½ cup red wine (bold
and fruity such as shiraz,
cabernet sauvignon, or
zinfandel)

Salt

Freshly ground
black pepper

1. Heat the olive oil in a medium sauté pan or skillet over a medium heat. Add the shallots and sauté for about 8 minutes, until they begin to soften and turn golden brown.

2. Add the sugar, thyme, and rosemary and caramelize the shallots for about 5 minutes, until they're browned.

3. Add the balsamic vinegar and red wine and continue to sauté for about 30 minutes, until the liquid has completely evaporated.

4. Remove the rosemary and thyme sprigs and add salt and pepper to taste.

5. Serve warm or let cool and refrigerate for up to 1 month.

Ingredient tip: These shallots are incredibly versatile on and off your cheese board. If you have leftovers, serve them with couscous and chicken, roasted meats, or over a warm salad of wilted greens. Add them to a grilled cheese sandwich for comfort food taken to the next level.

CANDIED BACON

MAKES 12 BACON SLICES / PREP TIME: 10 MINUTES / COOK TIME: 25 MINUTES, PLUS 15 MINUTES TO COOL

Candied bacon is fatty, crispy, sweet, and salty—in other words, pretty amazing. It provides a wonderful crunch to a cheese board and makes a terrific breakfast side, Bloody Mary garnish, or salad ingredient. Plus, there are only two ingredients, so why aren't you making this already?

**12 strips
thick-cut bacon**

½ cup light brown sugar

1. Preheat the oven to 350°F. Line a baking sheet with aluminum foil.

2. Put the sugar on a plate. Individually press each bacon strip into the sugar to coat on each side.

3. Arrange the sugar-coated bacon strips on a cooling rack on top of the prepared baking sheet. The cooling rack allows air to circulate, which helps crisp up the bacon and cook it evenly. If you don't have a cooling rack, you can place the bacon directly on the foil-lined tray, but be sure to leave a ½-inch space between the bacon slices to help them crisp evenly.

4. Place the tray in the center of the oven and bake for 20 to 25 minutes, or until the bacon is crispy and the sugar has completely melted.

5. Let cool for 10 to 15 minutes before serving. The bacon will keep in the refrigerator for 2 days.

Substitution tip: You can alter the number of bacon slices; just use two teaspoons of sugar per slice. You can also add herbs and spices to this bacon as desired, such as cayenne pepper, black pepper, or dried rosemary.

MAPLE-CAYENNE GLAZED NUTS

MAKES 2 CUPS / PREP TIME: 5 MINUTES / COOK TIME: 30 MINUTES, PLUS 15 MINUTES TO COOL

Maple syrup adds wonderful flavor to any candied ingredient. It's reminiscent of colder days, hot pancakes, and the woods. Add a little cayenne spice to break up the sweetness, and you've got the perfect treat. Hopefully you'll be able to save enough to put on your cheese board because it's hard to not keep snacking on these. Pecans are probably the most traditional nut to pair with maple, but walnuts, cashews, pistachios, or any of your favorites will work, too.

½ cup maple syrup

¼ teaspoon cayenne pepper

½ teaspoon vanilla extract

¼ teaspoon sea salt

2 cups nuts of your choice, such as pecans, walnuts, cashews, or pistachios

1. In a saucepan over medium-high heat, bring the syrup, cayenne pepper, vanilla, and sea salt to a boil, then reduce the heat to medium-low.

2. Add the nuts and stir to coat. Simmer for about 20 minutes, stirring frequently, until the liquid has almost completely evaporated and small crystals have begun to form on the nuts.

3. Transfer the nuts to a plate and use a spatula to break them up. Let cool for about 15 minutes.

4. Serve immediately, or store them in an airtight container at room temperature for up to 2 weeks.

Cooking tip: Real-deal maple syrup is graded by color and strength of flavor, ranging from a light and delicate flavor to a very dark color with a strong taste. For this recipe, try to use a grade A, dark color, and robust taste maple syrup, which has a strong enough maple flavor to balance the cayenne without over-powering it.

CANDIED NUTS

MAKES 4 CUPS / PREP TIME: 15 MINUTES / COOK TIME: 1 HOUR

Unlike glazed nuts, which are delightfully sticky, these nuts are easier to pop in your mouth one by one. They're incredibly versatile because they're just sweet, nutty, and crunchy, so you can add any other spices you'd like. Raw almonds make some of the best candied nuts, but go with your favorite.

1 teaspoon salt

1 teaspoon ground cinnamon

¾ cup sugar

1 tablespoon water

1 teaspoon vanilla extract

1 egg white

4 cups nuts of your choice, such as almonds or walnuts

1. Preheat the oven to 250°F. Line a baking sheet with parchment paper.

2. In a small bowl, mix together the salt, cinnamon, and sugar.

3. In a large bowl, combine the water, vanilla, and egg white and whisk until foamy.

4. Toss the nuts in the egg white froth to completely coat them. Slowly add the sugar mixture and combine completely.

5. Pour the nuts onto the prepared baking sheet and spread them out in one even layer.

6. Bake for 1 hour, stirring them every 15 minutes.

7. Allow the nuts to cool on the parchment paper. Serve immediately, or store them in an airtight container at room temperature for up to 2 weeks.

Cooking tip: Using egg whites to candy nuts works beautifully. The egg acts as a binder, so the sugar sticks more to the nuts than it does to your hand.

CANDIED LEMON PEEL

MAKES ABOUT ¾ CUP / PREP TIME: 15 MINUTES / COOK TIME: 2 HOURS

Candying raw citrus peel subdues its bitterness and tough texture, transforming it into a true treat. This process is also a fantastic way to use (rather than discard) your leftover lemon peels. On a cheese board, the candied peel adds color and texture and allows you to eat candy—but in a refined way.

4 lemons (preferably organic)

2 cups cold water, plus more to cover peel

2 cups granulated sugar

Nonstick cooking spray

¼ cup superfine sugar (optional)

1. Cut the lemons into quarters lengthwise and scoop out the insides. Use a sharp-edged spoon to remove the pith from the inside. Cut the peel pieces into ¼-inch-wide strips.

2. Put the lemon peels in a saucepan and cover them with water. Bring to a boil over medium-high heat, and then immediately drain. Return the lemon peels to the saucepan and repeat the boil and drain sequence once more. This repeated process removes the bitterness, but if you repeat it too many times, you'll lose the lemon flavor.

3. Return the twice-boiled lemon peels to the saucepan with 2 cups of cold water and the sugar. Bring to a boil over medium-high heat, stirring with a whisk to dissolve the sugar.

4. Reduce the heat to low and simmer for about 60 minutes, stirring occasionally, until the peels are mostly translucent.

5. While the peels are cooking, line a baking sheet with parchment paper and spray with cooking spray.

6. Drain the peels, reserving the sweet lemon syrup to use in cocktails and tea. Spread the peels out in an even layer on the baking sheet.

7. If desired, after cooling for about 10 minutes, until the peels have cooled enough to touch but are still soft and warm, dip each peel in the superfine sugar (if using) to coat for extra sweetness.

8. Let cool for at least 1 hour (3 hours if you coated them in sugar).

9. Store the candied peels in an airtight container for up to 3 weeks.

Substitution tip: Candied lemon peel is great with goat cheese, whereas orange peel works better with goudas. Try grapefruit peel with fresh farmer's cheese or ricotta.

ROASTED RED PEPPERS

MAKES ABOUT 2 CUPS / PREP TIME: 5 MINUTES / COOK TIME: 15 MINUTES

Roasted red peppers are extraordinarily easy to make and have deep flavors and vegetal sweetness. Chop them small and add them to hummus, or use them in a veggie wrap, pasta salad, or on an antipasto cheese board. Although you can buy roasted peppers at the store, the homemade version has an extra freshness and bright flavor.

2 large red bell peppers
(or as many as you'd like)

1 cup extra-virgin olive
oil (if storing)

1. Preheat the oven's broiler to 500°F. Line a baking sheet with aluminum foil.

2. Cut the red peppers in half lengthwise and remove the caps, stems, and flesh. Place them skin-side up on the prepared baking sheet.

3. Bake on the top rack near the broiler for 10 to 15 minutes, until the skins look loose in places and are charred black.

4. Using oven mitts, pull the foil up around the peppers to create a pouch to lock in the heat, and steam them for another 10 minutes.

5. As soon as the peppers are cool enough to handle, pull the skins off; they should slide off easily.

6. Cut the peppers into strips lengthwise and serve, or cover them in the olive oil and store them in the refrigerator for up to 2 weeks.

Cooking tip: You can also roast peppers directly on a gas stovetop. It's a bit messy, and you can only roast one pepper at a time, but it produces a great smoky flavor. Place a pepper directly on the burner, turn the flame to medium high, and cook for 4 to 5 minutes on each side, rotating with tongs, until the pepper is charred all over—about 20 minutes total.

CORNICHON AND ONION RELISH

MAKES ABOUT 1 CUP / PREP TIME: 10 MINUTES

Cornichons are a classic accompaniment to cheese. They're tiny French pickles made from gherkin cucumbers that are picked before reaching maturity, so they're cute and small, just about an inch long with a bright tartness and real crunch. This simple recipe retains the crisp texture, adds flavor, and makes it easier to enjoy cornichons in a smaller bite with cheese and bread.

½ cup diced cornichons

¼ cup finely diced sweet onion

3 tablespoons minced flat-leaf parsley

2 teaspoons cornichon juice

1 tablespoon Dijon mustard

⅛ teaspoon freshly ground black pepper

In a small bowl, combine all the ingredients and toss. Store the relish in the refrigerator for up to 1 month.

Ingredient tip: If you have leftovers of this relish, use it to take the place of both mustard and pickles in a sandwich, mix it into a chicken salad, or serve it with pork chops. Leftover whole cornichons can be martini or Bloody Mary garnishes.

CARAMEL PEARS

Fully caramelized pears are a dream dessert but are a bit sticky and messy to eat with cheese. By briefly broiling the pear, you begin to caramelize the sugars but not enough for the pear to fall apart. To highlight the cooked-sugar flavor, these lightly baked pears are dipped in caramel. If you have extra caramel, you can add it straight to your cheese board or use it in a number of desserts.

2 pears (Barlett or D'Anjou are best)

1 tablespoon freshly squeezed lemon juice

1 tablespoon brown sugar

½ cup sugar

½ cup water

¼ cup heavy (whipping) cream, at room temperature

3 tablespoons salted butter, cubed, at room temperature

1. Preheat the oven's broiler to 500°F.

2. Remove the stems from the pears and core them, then cut them into ¼-inch-thick slices.

3. Lightly brush the lemon juice on the pear slices, then evenly and lightly sprinkle the brown sugar on top.

4. Put the slices on a broiling pan and broil on the top shelf of the oven for about 4 minutes. Remove once the tops of the pears begin to brown. Set aside.

5. In a medium saucepan over medium-high heat, combine the sugar and water and whisk until the sugar has dissolved.

6. Once the sugar has completely dissolved, stop whisking and cook for about 5 minutes, or until it becomes amber in color.

7. Whisk in the cream to stop the caramel from cooking and burning, then add the butter and continue to stir until the texture is smooth.

8. Remove from the heat and cool for about 10 minutes. Dip each pear slice in the caramel and serve.

Ingredient tip: Caramel pears work as a standalone dessert, or you can serve them with bread pudding, on a yogurt parfait with granola, or in an almond tart.

WINE-POACHED CHERRIES

MAKES 2 CUPS / PREP TIME: 5 MINUTES / COOK TIME: 30 MINUTES

Cherry and wine make a wonderful marriage because so many fruit-forward wines have a natural cherry note to them. Try a young Tempranillo or a fruity merlot to bring out those flavors. This recipe uses dried cherries because they won't be as mushy and runny as fresh cherries, and they also offer a little more tartness. Poached cherries are a great complement to already sweet cheeses, like gouda, and can stand up to a spicy blue.

2 cups dry fruity
red wine

1 cup water

2 tablespoons sugar

3 tablespoons honey

1 teaspoon
vanilla extract

2 whole cloves

1 cinnamon stick

1½ cups dried tart
cherries

1. In a medium saucepan over medium-high heat, combine the wine, water, and sugar and bring to a boil, whisking to dissolve the sugar.

2. Whisk in the honey, and then reduce the heat to medium low. Bring to a simmer and add the vanilla, cloves, and cinnamon. Simmer for 5 minutes.

3. Add the cherries and simmer for 15 to 20 minutes, until they're soft and plump and the liquid has reduced and become syrupy.

4. Remove the cloves and cinnamon and drain the cherries. It's easier to eat the cherries with cheese if they're drained, but if you prefer, pour the syrup over the cherries for a more preserves-like consistency.

5. Serve immediately, or store them in the refrigerator for 2 days.

Food pairing: Wine-poached cherries are not only wonderful with a myriad of cheeses, but they also make a striking topper to many desserts, such as cheesecake, ice cream, and, of course, cherry pie.

BALSAMIC ARTICHOKES

MAKES 24 BITES / PREP TIME: 1 HOUR / COOK TIME: 15 MINUTES

Baby artichokes are wonderful because you can eat the whole flower, unlike a regular artichoke, which has to be completely cleaned. They have an earthy and nutty flavor, similar to asparagus with a mild bitterness. The artichoke occupies a special place in the cheese world because its cousin, the bull thistle, is used in place of rennet to coagulate certain traditional cheeses from Portugal and Italy.

8 baby artichokes

3 tablespoons balsamic vinegar

1 tablespoon freshly squeezed lemon juice

½ cup extra-virgin olive oil

½ teaspoon salt

½ teaspoon freshly ground black pepper

1. Trim the artichoke stems and remove any hard outer leaves. Cut the top quarter off each artichoke and cut them lengthwise into quarters.

2. In a gallon-size resealable bag, combine the balsamic vinegar, lemon juice, olive oil, salt, and pepper. Seal the bag, and then shake it to mix thoroughly. Open the bag, add the artichokes, close the bag, and shake it again to coat. Let the artichokes marinate in the bag at room temperature for 30 minutes to 1 hour.

3. Heat a grill pan on medium-high heat and lay the artichokes on the pan, leaf-side down. Grill for 4 to 5 minutes on each side, until charred.

4. Serve and enjoy warm or at room temperature.

Cooking tip: As with any grilled food, these artichokes are best served immediately, but, if necessary, they can be stored for up to two days in a food-safe container in the refrigerator.

DRIED BLOOD ORANGES

MAKES ABOUT 15 SLICES / PREP TIME: 10 MINUTES / COOK TIME: 2 HOURS

Blood oranges are stunning, adding a dazzling pop of ruby red to a cheese board. They're typically most available in the winter months, bringing a much needed brightness during that cold and dark time of year. Although fresh citrus fruits, such as grapefruit and oranges, can be a bit too sour for cheese, these dried and crispy beauties are mellower while adding the perfect amount of zing.

2 blood oranges

½ teaspoon ground ginger

¼ teaspoon ground nutmeg

¼ cup raw sugar

1. Preheat the oven to 200°F. Line two baking sheets with parchment paper.

2. Wash and dry the oranges and slice them as thin and evenly as possible, no more than ⅛ inch thick. Use a mandolin if you have one to ensure evenness.

3. In a small bowl, mix together the ginger, nutmeg, and sugar. Sprinkle the mixture evenly on both sides of each orange slice.

4. Arrange the slices on the prepared baking sheets in a single layer, so they're not touching one another, and place the trays on the bottom rack of the oven.

5. Bake for 1 hour, flip the slices, and then bake for 1 hour more. If the orange slices are not fully dehydrated, leave them in the oven for another 30 minutes, or until they are fully dried through.

6. Let cool and serve.

Ingredient tip: Dried blood oranges make fabulous cocktail garnishes, or you can add them to your morning cereal. They also go beautifully with baked fish or chicken. And by dehydrating them, you'll be able to eat the rind, too.

BAKED BUTTERNUT SQUASH CHIPS

MAKES ABOUT 2½ CUPS / PREP TIME: 10 MINUTES / COOK TIME: 40 MINUTES

Butternut squash chips are a healthier alternative to potato chips, but the benefits don't stop there. These chips have sweet and nutty flavors and take well to herbs. They're nicely crunchy and works well on any cheese board. Plus, if you're watching your carbs or are just tired of bread and crackers with every board, these chips also work as a vehicle for the cheese itself.

1 medium
butternut squash

1 tablespoon extra-virgin
olive oil

½ teaspoon kosher salt

1 teaspoon chopped
fresh rosemary

1 teaspoon chopped
fresh sage

1. Preheat the oven to 350°F. Line two baking sheets with parchment paper.

2. Remove the stem from the butternut squash and cut it in half lengthwise.

3. Place the cut side of each squash half on a cutting board, and cut thin and even slices starting from the neck, about ⅛ inch thick. If you have a mandolin, you can use that, but it's important to get evenly thick slices. You may wish to cut the slices from the bulbous part of the squash in half again, so they are all close in size.

4. In a bowl, toss the squash slices with the olive oil, salt, rosemary, and sage.

5. Lay the squash slices in a single layer on each of the prepared baking sheets.

6. Bake for about 40 minutes, checking every 10 minutes to make sure the slices don't burn, and flipping after 20 minutes. Let cool and serve.

Substitution tip: Butternut squash is reminiscent of fall flavors, but you can substitute other vegetables in this recipe; just be sure to check on them regularly because different vegetables will cook at different speeds. Try beets for an earthy tang, carrots for roasted sweetness, or turnips for a mild woodsy flavor.

WATER CRACKERS

MAKES ABOUT 30 CRACKERS / PREP TIME: 15 MINUTES / COOK TIME: 15 MINUTES

Water crackers may be the ultimate vehicle to transport cheese from the board to your mouth. They have a very subtle flavor, so they won't interrupt the curated cheeses and pairings you've worked so hard to achieve. Sure, you can buy crackers at the store, but these homemade crackers will taste even better and will impress everyone; just don't tell them how easy they are to make!

1 cup flour

½ teaspoon kosher salt

2 tablespoons olive oil

¼ cup water, plus more if needed

1. Preheat the oven to 375°F. Line a baking sheet with parchment paper.

2. In a food processor, mix the flour and salt. Set the food processor to low and slowly add the olive oil, then slowly pour in the water as the processor mixes. The resulting mixture will be grainy and only slightly sticky but soft enough to form a ball without breaking apart. If the flour is still too dry to form a ball, add more water, 1 tablespoon at a time.

3. Form the dough into a ball but do not knead it.

4. On a lightly floured surface, roll the dough out with a rolling pin as thinly and evenly as possible. Using a sharp knife or pizza slicer, cut the dough into small rectangular crackers, about 1-by-2-inches, or in any shape you desire.

5. Brush off any excess flour and transfer the dough to the prepared baking sheet and bake for 10 to 15 minutes, or until lightly golden on the edges.

6. Let cool and serve.

Cooking tip: These crackers have good crunch but are purposefully very mild to let your cheese shine. Feel free to play with flavors that pair with your cheeses, too. You can add nearly anything to these crackers, such as sesame seeds, cracked black pepper, chopped fresh rosemary, or chives. Adding half a teaspoon of most spices, herbs, and seeds will give you just enough flavor without overwhelming the cracker.

CHEESE GLOSSARY

CHEESE	STYLE	TASTE	SUBSTITUTION(S) OR BRAND(S)	RECIPE(S)
Alp Blossom	Hard, Alpine	Colorful, herbaceous, flowery, savory, nutty		Springtime Bloom (page 47)
Appenzeller	Hard, Alpine	Herbs, grassy, floral, savory	Substitutions: Challerhocker, Murray's Annelies	Bold and Strong (page 38)
Asiago d'Allevo	Hard, Italian	Sweet, mild, milky, fresh, supple, semisoft	Substitutions: Sartori Extra-Aged Asiago, Saputo Asiago	Italian Antipasto (page 53)
Barely Buzzed	Hard	Espresso, caramel, lavender, toasted nuts	Brand: Beehive	Cream and Coffee (page 72)
Basque, Mini	Semi-firm, Basque	Dense, buttery, nutty, smooth, mildly wooly		Try It All (page 57)
BellaVitano, Bourbon	Hard, Italian	Vanilla, caramel, bourbon barrels, crunchy crystals studded in smooth cream	Substitutions: Occelli Barley Malt and Whiskey	Nutty and Honeyed Cheeses (page 66)
BellaVitano, Espresso	Hard, Italian	Coffee, roasted, dark chocolate, sweet cream, whole milk		Cream and Coffee (page 72)
Black Ash	Vegan	Buttery, sweet, mild tang, dense	Miyoko's	Vegan Cheeses (page 34)
Blue, Bayley Hazen	Blue	Dense, grassy, light pepper, mild blue funk, toasted nuts	Brand: Jasper Hill; Substitutions: Devon Blue, Stilton	Date Night Dessert (page 64); Nutty and Honeyed Cheeses (page 66)
Blue, Cashel	Blue	Buttery, floral, creamy, herbaceous, hay, spicy, white peppercorn		Springtime Bloom (page 47) Try It All (page 57)
Blue, Danish	Blue	Lactic, moist, soft, light hay, salty		Cream and Caramel (page 67)
Blue, Middlebury	Blue	Black pepper, hay, light caramel, spicy		For a Dinner Roast (page 41)

CHEESE	STYLE	TASTE	SUBSTITUTION(S) OR BRAND(S)	RECIPE(S)
Blue, Saint Agur	Blue	Luscious, creamy, moist, dense, tangy, subtle spice	Substitution: Bleu d'Auvergne	Winter Warmth (page 49)
Blue, Shropshire	Blue	Tangy, sharp, slightly spicy, creamy, crumbly	Substitution: Butlers Blacksticks Blue	Rainbow Board (page 61) I Love Blue (page 69)
Blue French Style Sheese, Bute Island	Vegan	Peppery, pleasant bitterness	Brand: Bute Island	Vegan Cheeses (page 34)
Brie, Sheep	Soft-ripened, bloomy rind	Buttery, milky, soft, pillowy	Substitutions: Brebirousse d'Argental, Old Chatham Creamery Hudson Valley Camembert, Murray's Brebis Noir	Winter Warmth (page 49)
Brillat-Savarin	Soft-ripened, bloomy rind, triple crème	Unctuous, heavy cream, intensely buttery, opulent	Substitutions: Cremeux de Bourgogne, Délice de Bourgogne, Four Fat Fowl St. Stephen	Decadence and Bubbles (page 52) Chocolate and Cheese (page 68)
Burrata	Fresh, pasta filata	Creamy, gooey, delicately decadent	Brands: Maplebrook Farm, Narragansett Creamery, Caputo Creamery	Fresh Burrata Caprese (page 36)
Cabrales	Blue	Piquant, pungent, peppery, wet leaves, spicy	Substitution: Valdéon	Bold and Strong (page 38)
Cambozola Black Label	Soft-ripened, bloomy rind, blue	Soft, butter bomb, mild mushroom, sweet nuts		I Love Blue (page 69)
Camembert	Soft-ripened, bloomy rind	Mushroom, earthy, hay, buttery	Brand: Marin French	Farm and Field (page 42) Earth and Smoke (page 55)
Capra Verde	Hard	Fudgy, peppery, light sharpness, lemony	Substitutions: Montchèvre Chèvre in Blue, Lively Run Cayuga Blue	Goat Three Ways (page 37)
Casatica	Soft-ripened, bloomy rind	Rich, decadent, whole milk, sweet	Substitution: Nuvola di Pecora	For a Dinner Roast (page 41)

CHEESE	STYLE	TASTE	SUBSTITUTION(S) OR BRAND(S)	RECIPE(S)
Cheddar, Farmhouse	Hard	Toasted nuts, Dijon mustard, grassy	Brands: Beecher's Flagship, Jasper Hill Cave Aged Cheddar, Tillamook Extra Sharp Cheddar, Cabot Clothbound, Murray's Stockinghall	Farmhouse Cheddar and Butter Board (page 33)
Cheddar, Flory's Truckle	Hard, cheddar	Grassy, hay, horseradish, mustard, rich		Made in the USA (page 60)
Cheddar, Grafton	Hard, cheddar	Sharp tangy, creamy, buttery, nutty		Summer Freshness (page 51)
Cheddar, Guinness	Hard, cheddar	Butterscotch, chocolate, dried apricots		Beer Lover's Board (page 39)
Cheddar, Irish	Hard, cheddar	Grassy, fruity, sweet, acidic, crumbly		Winter Warmth (page 49) Fan Favorites (page 56)
Chèvre, Honey-Flavored	Fresh	Fresh and tangy, balanced sweetness		Fall Flavors (page 46)
Chèvre Log	Fresh	Creamy, bright, tangy, smooth	Brands: Laura Chenel, Goat Lady Dairy, Vermont Creamery	Summer Freshness (page 51)
Comté, Aged	Hard, Alpine	Roasted nuts, sautéed onion, yolky, cauliflower	Substitution: Gruyère	Decadence and Bubbles (page 52)
Cremont	Soft-ripened, bloomy rind	Soft, creamy, cloud-like, cakey, pleasant tang	Brand: Vermont Creamery Substitution: Vermont Creamery Coupole	Made in the USA (page 60)
Époisses	Soft-ripened, washed rind	Meaty, intense, bacony, salt		Bold and Strong (page 38)
Farmer's Cheese	Fresh	Fresh, lactic, smooth, creamy, mild	Buy local!	Nutty and Honeyed Cheeses (page 66)
Fontina Val d'Aosta	Hard, Italian, Alpine	Smooth, earthy, toasted cashew, supple, mild truffle mushroom		Mushroom Mania (page 70)
Fourme d'Ambert	Blue	Less spicy blue, rich, decadent, sweet cream, velvety		French Fromage (page 65)

CHEESE	STYLE	TASTE	SUBSTITUTION(S) OR BRAND(S)	RECIPE(S)
Gorgonzola, Mountain	Blue	Spicy, crumbly, salty, peppery, earthy		Earth and Smoke (page 55)
Gorgonzola Cremificato	Blue	Creamy, fudgy, spicy, tangy		Fall Flavors (page 46)
Gorgonzola Dolce	Blue	Sweet, fatty, light sour cream		Summer Freshness (page 51) I Love Blue (page 69)
Gouda, Ewephoria	Hard, gouda	Candied nuts, butterscotch, caramel, firm, sugar		Cream and Caramel (page 67)
Gouda, Extra Aged	Hard, gouda	Firm, flaky, dry, crumbly, whiskey, pecan pie	Brands: Beemster, Boerenkaas Aged 24 Months, Fourmage, Two Sisters Isabella Gouda, Marieke Aged Raw Milk Gouda	Chocolate and Cheese (page 68)
Gouda, Goat	Hard, gouda	Sweet, caramel, mild acidity, satin texture	Brands: Balarina, L'Amuse Brabander, Central Coast Creamery, Beemster	Goat Three Ways (page 37)
Gouda, Smoked	Hard, gouda	Smoky, buttery, hickory, sweet		Earth and Smoke (page 55) Made in the USA (page 60)
Gouda, Young	Hard, gouda	Caramel, cooked cream, springy	Brand: Beemster Gouda Light	Beer Lover's Board (page 39) Fan Favorites (page 56)
Gouda Roomano	Hard, gouda	Firm, deep sweetness, light sharpness, crystal crunch		Cream and Coffee (page 72)
Gran Queso	Hard	Firm, cinnamon-sweetness, subdued sharpness, mildly oily	Substitution: Alisios	Winter Warmth (page 49)
Gruyère	Hard, Alpine	Creamy, hay, nutty, savory, caramel	Substitution: Comté	Rainbow Board (page 61)

CHEESE	STYLE	TASTE	SUBSTITUTION(S) OR BRAND(S)	RECIPE(S)
Harbison	Soft-ripened, bloomy rind	Funky, earthy, woodsy	Brand: Jasper Hill Substitutions: Vacherin Mont d'Or, Jasper Hill Winnimere, Uplands Rush Creek Reserve	Fall Flavors (page 46)
Hudson Flower	Soft-ripened, bloomy rind	Creamy, earthy, floral	Brand: Murray's Cave-master Reserve Substitution: Monet Chèvre with Flowers	Springtime Bloom (page 47)
Humboldt Fog	Soft-ripened, bloomy rind	Goaty, citric, herbaceous, chalky, powdery	Brand: Cypress Grove	Try It All (page 57)
Idiazabal	Hard	Woodsy, bacony, caramel, smoky	Substitution: Roncal, Zamorano	Spanish Tapas (page 35)
Langres	Soft-ripened, bloomy rind, washed rind	Soft, pungent, melt-in-your-mouth, complex, wrinkled rind	Substitution: Jasper Hill Willoughby	French Fromage (page 65)
La Tur	Soft-ripened, bloomy rind	Soft, cake batter, fresh cream, tangy	Substitutions: Nettle Meadow Kunik, Jasper Hill, Little Hosmer	Italian Antipasto (page 53)
Limburger	Soft-ripened, washed rind	Meaty, savory, umami, salty	Substitutions: Meadow Creek Dairy Grayson, Bachensteiner	Farm and Field (page 42)
Manchego, Aged	Hard	Firm, buttery, rustic	Brands: 1605, Mitica, El Trigal	Spanish Tapas (page 35) Fall Flavors (page 46)
Manchego, Young	Hard	Creamy, supple, grassy, slight sharpness		Fan Favorites (page 56) Rainbow Board (page 61)
Meule de Savoie	Hard, Alpine	Firm, fruity, toasted nuts, hay, cooked cream	Substitutions: Jasper Hill Alpha Tolman, Uplands Pleasant Ridge Reserve	Summer Freshness (page 51)
Mimolette	Hard	Caramel, dense, firm, oily, fruity, nutty		Earth and Smoke (page 55)
Monte Enebro	Soft-ripened, blue	Soft, chalky, tangy, minerally	Substitutions: Westfield Farm Classic Blue, Leonora	Spanish Tapas (page 35)
Monterey Jack, Dry	Hard	Aged, firm, nutty, assertive, dry	Recommended brand: Vella	Made in the USA (page 60)

CHEESE	STYLE	TASTE	SUBSTITUTION(S) OR BRAND(S)	RECIPE(S)
Nut Cheese, Classic Aged	Vegan	Smoky, mild, creamy	Brand: Treeline	Vegan Cheeses (page 34)
Ossau-Iraty	Hard, Basque	Wooly, firm, cashew, hazelnut, cooked cream	Substitutions: Garrotxa, Pyrénées Brebis	Winter Warmth (page 49)
Parmigiano-Reggiano Stravecchio	Hard, Italian	Savory, full, salty, tangy, golden, crunchy crystals	Substitution: Sartori SarVecchio	Try It All (page 57)
Pecorino, Truffle	Hard, pecorino	Truffle, mushroom, olive oil, earthy		Mushroom Mania (page 70)
Pecorino Oro Antico	Hard, pecorino	Olive oil, wooly, firm, flaky, salty, butterfat, nutty		Date Night Dessert (page 64)
Pecorino Toscano	Hard, pecorino	Savory sweet balance, salty, peppery, sweet fruit, compact texture	Substitution: Fiore Sardo	Italian Antipasto (page 53)
Pont L'Évêque	Soft-ripened, washed rind	Soft, barnyardy, aromatic, apple orchard, pleasant		Try It All (page 57)
Provolone, Aged	Hard, pasta filata	Robust, firm, spicy, piquant, salty	Substitution: Parish Hill Suffolk Punch	Italian Antipasto (page 53)
Quadrello di Bufala	Soft-ripened, washed rind	Sweet, grassy, creamy, earthy, mushroom, hay, fudgy		Decadence and Bubbles (page 52)
Raclette	Hard, Alpine	Hazelnut, spring onion, almond, grassy	Substitutions: Spring Brook Farm Reading, Haystack Mountain Snowmass Raclette, Emmentaler	For a Dinner Roast (page 41)
Ricotta, Fresh	Fresh	Mild sweetness, smooth, soft, fresh, whey		Summer Freshness (page 51)
Robiola	Soft-ripened, bloomy rind	Delicate, mild, sweet, creamy, soft, graceful		Fan Favorites (page 56)
Roquefort	Blue	Spicy, salty, moist, rich	Recommended brand: Papillon	I Love Blue (page 69)

CHEESE	STYLE	TASTE	SUBSTITUTION(S) OR BRAND(S)	RECIPE(S)
Sainte Maure	Soft-ripened, ash	Fresh, yeasty, tangy, soft, grassy	Substitution: Selles-Sur-Cher, Vermont Creamery Bonne Bouche	Goat Three Ways (page 37) French Fromage (page 65)
Stilton	Blue	Chocolate, crumbly, creamy, tangy, distinctive spice	Recommended brand: Colsten-Bassett	Chocolate and Cheese (page 68)
Taleggio	Soft-ripened, washed rind	Fruity, pungent, dense, sweet, creamy, funky	Substitutions: Grey Barn Prufrock, von Trapp Creamery Oma	Italian Antipasto (page 53) Earth and Smoke (page 55)
Tête de Moine	Semi-firm, Alpine	Roasted nuts, pungent, smooth		Springtime Bloom (page 47)
Toma Piemontese	Semi-firm, tomme	Smooth, sweet nuts, cooked cream, lightly woodsy	Substitutions: Toma di Gressoney, Tomme de Savoie	Rainbow Board (page 61)
Tomme Brûlée	Semi-firm, tomme	Butterscotch, brown butter, roasted nuts, smoky, dense		Cream and Caramel (page 67)
Tomme de Savoie	Semi-firm, tomme	Minerally, cave, nutty, lactic	Substitution: Tomme de Crayeuse	Farm and Field (page 42)
Up In Smoke	Fresh	Smoky, bright, autumn, leaf-wrapped	Brand: River's Edge Substitutions: Capriole O'Banon, Caciotta Capra Foglie de Noce	Beer Lover's Board (page 39)
Valençay	Soft-ripened, ash rind	Tangy, hay, goaty, citric, chalky yet creamy	Substitutions: Country Winds Ashed Pyramid, Mont Idyll, Yellow Springs Farm Black Diamond	Rainbow Board (page 61)

MEASUREMENT CONVERSIONS

1 POUND CHEESE = 16 OUNCES, SERVES 11 TO 15 PEOPLE

Volume Equivalents (Liquid)

US STANDARD	US STANDARD (OUNCES)	METRIC (APPROXIMATE)
2 tablespoons	1 fl. oz.	30 mL
¼ cup	2 fl. oz.	60 mL
½ cup	4 fl. oz.	120 mL
1 cup	8 fl. oz.	240 mL
1½ cups	12 fl. oz.	355 mL
2 cups or 1 pint	16 fl. oz.	475 mL
4 cups or 1 quart	32 fl. oz.	1 L
1 gallon	128 fl. oz.	4 L

Oven Temperatures

FAHRENHEIT	CELSIUS (APPROXIMATE)
250°F	120°C
300°F	150°C
325°F	165°C
350°F	180°C
375°F	190°C
400°F	200°C
425°F	220°C
450°F	230°C

Volume Equivalents (Dry)

US STANDARD	METRIC (APPROXIMATE)
⅛ teaspoon	0.5 mL
¼ teaspoon	1 mL
½ teaspoon	2 mL
¾ teaspoon	4 mL
1 teaspoon	5 mL
1 tablespoon	15 mL
¼ cup	59 mL
⅓ cup	79 mL
½ cup	118 mL
⅔ cup	156 mL
¾ cup	177 mL
1 cup	235 mL
2 cups or 1 pint	475 mL
3 cups	700 mL
4 cups or 1 quart	1 L

Weight Equivalents

US STANDARD	METRIC (APPROXIMATE)
½ ounce	15 g
1 ounce	30 g
2 ounces	60 g
4 ounces	115 g
8 ounces	225 g
12 ounces	340 g
16 ounces or 1 pound	455 g

RESOURCES

INTRO TO CHEESE BOOKS

The Book of Cheese: The Essential Guide to Discovering Cheeses You'll Love by Liz Thorpe

Cheese and Culture: A History of Cheese and its Place in Western Civilization by Paul Kindstedt

Cheese Primer by Steven Jenkins

The Oxford Companion to Cheese by Catherine Donnelly and Mateo Kehler

ONLINE CHEESE RESOURCES

American Cheese Society CheeseSociety.org

Cheese Science Toolkit CheeseScience.org

Culture Cheese Magazine CultureCheeseMag.com

Oldways Cheese Coalition OldwaysPT.org/programs/oldways-cheese-coalition

BUYING CHEESE ONLINE

Artisanal Premium Cheese ArtisanalCheese.com

Formaggio Kitchen FormaggioKitchen.com/cheese

iGourmet iGourmet.com

Murray's Cheese MurraysCheese.com

CHEESEMAKING 101

Artisan Cheese Making at Home: Techniques & Recipes for Mastering World-Class Cheeses by Mary Karlin

Kitchen Creamery: Making Yogurt, Butter & Cheese at Home by Louella Hill

The Beginner's Guide to Cheese Making: Easy Recipes and Lessons to Make Your Own Handcrafted Cheeses by Elena R. Santogade

BEER RESOURCES

Cheese & Beer by Janet Fletcher

The Brewmaster's Table: Discovering the Pleasures of Real Beer with Real Food by Garrett Oliver

WINE RESOURCES

Cheese & Wine: A Guide to Selecting, Pairing, and Enjoying by Janet Fletcher

The Wine Bible by Karen MacNeil

Wine Folly WineFolly.com

INDEX

ACKNOWLEDGMENTS

Thanks to my partner, Philip Hensley, who inspires me to follow my passions and helps me translate cheese into words through tasting my pairings, finding the right phrases, and supporting and loving me in every way.

Thanks to my sister, Karen Adler, for whom this book is written. Her writing and editing skills are unparalleled. Thanks to my mom, Peggy Robin, for being my author role model, and for being the best. And to my dad, who made sure I always had cheesy snacks as a kid, even if it was mostly Boursin and Laughing Cow.

Thanks to my editor, Laura Apperson, and the entire team at Callisto for trusting my writing and expertise and making this process as smooth as possible.

Thanks to my best friends, Leah Pierson, Nina Khoury, and Bo Malin-Mayor, for always loving me and not thinking I was crazy to pursue cheese. Thanks to my classmates at Temple University for their additional daily support.

Thanks to all my friends, past and present, at Tria for teaching me, listening to my weekly nerdy ramblings about cheese, and providing me with room for growth, with special thanks to Sarafina Kietzman-Nicklin, Jacki Philleo, and Leah Blewett.

Thanks to all the cheese educators, makers, and mongers, especially the local Philly-area cheesemakers and mongers who accepted me into their cheesy world.

ABOUT THE AUTHOR

CLAIRE ROBIN ADLER is an American Cheese Society Certified Cheese Professional (ACS CCP®) based in Philadelphia. She worked as the Cheese Director for a group of four wine bars where she curated and created delicious cheese boards, as well as taught cheese classes. She currently works as a cheese educator and consultant, creating perfect pairings and boards for chefs, restaurants, and caterers, and offers private cheese classes.

CPSIA information can be obtained
at www.ICGtesting.com
Printed in the USA
JSHW041714050721
16602JS00004B/138